Tsunami!

from a few that survived

ISBN:1-885270-59-3

Cover Design: Kristi Yoder and Rachel Mast

First Printing: September 2006

Second Printing: October 2006

Printed in the USA

For more information about Christian Aid Ministries, see pages 146-147.

To order additional copies of *Tsunami!* please contact:

TGS International
PO Box 355
Berlin, Ohio 44610 USA
Phone: 330·893·2428
Fax: 330·893·2305

CAM061023AM1
HG12058

Tsunami!

from a few that survived

by Harvey Yoder

Table of Contents

Dedication

CAM has been involved in many international crisis projects, but what we saw when we arrived in Indonesia on January 14, 2005, seemed almost beyond our ability to fathom. Truckloads of bodies were still being delivered to a mass grave at the edge of the city of *Banda Aceh,** Indonesia. The smell of death hung heavy in the air. Devastation and destruction stretched as far as the eye could see. Banda Aceh, a city of 425,000 close to the epicenter of the monster quake, lost approximately 80,000 of its people.

God's ways are not our ways. Job tells us God ". . . doeth great things past finding out; yea, and wonders without number."

Banda Aceh is located on the island of Sumatra, Indonesia. Prior to the tsunami, this area was almost totally closed to people from the West and to Christianity. This tragedy yielded new opportunities to be "salt" and "light" in an area almost 100 percent Muslim. Most of what the people in this area knew about Christianity was drawn from their knowledge of America, and that came from their exposure to ungodly Hollywood films.

God opened a window of opportunity to change this perception and to portray the love of Christ to grieving survivors, many of whom lost everything they had on this earth, including family. Hundreds of volunteers from North America left the comfort of hearth and home and traveled to this remote spot to rebuild houses and to witness and testify for Jesus. Doors were also flung open to distribute hundreds of thousands of Bible story books. It is our earnest prayer—and we invite you to pray with us—that souls there could be won for the Kingdom. If even one soul from Banda Aceh will be in heaven as a result of this project, all the efforts will be more than worth it.

* Refer to glossary on page 143 for pronunciations of italicized words.

We dedicate this book to each of the brave, compassionate volunteers who took time off from work, paid their own tickets, and flew halfway around the world to help build God's kingdom there.

David N. Troyer
General Director
Christian Aid Ministries
September 2006

Preface

Thousands of stories emerged from the rubble of the devastating earthquake and tsunami that hit the eastern hemisphere on December 26, 2004. The following stories are just a very, very few, gleaned from several survivors in Banda Aceh.

Why choose these stories? Why not focus on some of the more spectacular rescues or zoom in on the hundreds of thousands of people who perished? What is special about these?

It is difficult to comprehend disasters if we merely read statistics and see faces in photographs. But if we can enter someone's life, feel his human emotions, and then follow him through a tragedy, we get a different glimpse of the catastrophe.

This is what I have tried to do with the following stories. I have chosen, for the most part, ordinary people whose lives were interrupted by one of the greatest natural disasters in history. These people, like all of us, had families, jobs, and homes and lived in communities. Their customs and language are different from ours, and even their ideals and ways of thinking might be strange to the Western world; yet I hope we can see that all humans, wherever we live, have the same basic needs of shelter, food, and protection from the elements.

I also chose these people for a special reason. Most of the people I interviewed either were Christians before the tsunami or became Christians after the tsunami. I wanted to show what believing in Christ really does for people who face a disaster.

Most of us face some personal "tsunami" in one way or another—the death of someone in the family, the disappointment of a loved one losing faith in God, a disaster such as losing a home to fire, or some other great financial loss.

In all of these, what do we do? Can we put our faith to the test and say with Job, "Though he slay me, yet will I trust in him"?

People told me about unusual events. Some spoke of seeing flocks of birds flying swiftly away from the ocean before the tsunami hit. Others told tales of elephants stampeding away from the killer waves. Surely the earth was groaning in agony as it was being ripped apart.

The stories kept piling up. Six women climbed a giant, spreading tree within sight of the ocean, clambering up and up as the water rose, clinging desperately to the very top of the branches while the wave swept death over the land. I saw the tree and tried to imagine the terror of those women.

Two sisters were helping their grandmother run away from the wall of water. When the water hit the back of their legs, the grandmother pleaded with them to go on and save themselves. The girls refused. When the wave lifted them up and pushed them against a metal gate, they saw their grandmother's grip slipping. They quickly tied her to the gate with some of their clothing, and the old woman and the girls survived the flood.

One family, desperate to get their old patriarch to safety, tried to flag down speeding motorcycles to put their grandfather on the back. One cyclist had to slow down, and a dozen hands reached out to stop him. They refused to let him go until the driver agreed to take the old man with him.

More than once, the survivors talked about the trauma of hearing people cry for help but being powerless to provide assistance. The cries of the hurt and dying haunt them to this day.

To the many who shared their experiences and stories with me, I thank you. To the group of young people who helped organize our schedule and made it possible to collect the stories, God bless you richly.

To all those from Christian Aid Ministries who made it possible for me to collect the information I needed to write this book, thank you.

Thank you, most of all, Jesus Christ, for the strength you poured into your children during this time. May the testimonies of your children continue to inspire all the believers.

—Harvey Yoder, 2006

Introduction

One minute and several seconds before eight o'clock on Sunday morning, December 26, 2004, about one hundred miles west of the Island of Sumatra, the India Plate and the Burma Plate collided with terrific force, heaving the ocean floor upward in a swift, mighty eruption about eighteen miles below the ocean's surface. This huge earthquake, registering over nine on the ten-point Richter scale, made enormous changes on the floor of the ocean. Gigantic rocks weighing millions of tons were dragged as much as seven miles across the ocean floor, and massive landslides occurred as the seabed cascaded into chasms. The tremor, if you can call such a quake a tremor, is thought to have caused the earth to wobble as it rotated on its axis. So great was the movement that islands were moved as much as sixty feet as the plates slid over each other.

This massive quake not only heaved up the sea floor, but also split open the earth in other places. It is estimated that seven cubic miles of water under the Indian Ocean were displaced. It was this violent displacement of the sea that caused the tsunami.

As the seawater was heaved upward, it caused a gigantic trough on either side of the upheaval, causing the waters to recede from the coastlines. As the waters receded, miles of beaches were exposed all along the low-lying areas of the countries close to the epicenter of the quake.

For some people, out early in the morning, this was disastrous. Reveling in the oddity of the ocean exposing its floor, they ran out to explore the beds of coral and catch the fish in the shallow pools. Hundreds of feet from the sandy shore, they were not at all prepared for the imminent danger.

Water rushing away from the shore in unprecedented volumes can mean only one thing. A massive earthquake has opened up the earth and the ocean is pouring into the cavities, filling all voids with tremendous movement and force. When the sea began emptying itself into the gigantic crack, it affected the entire ocean for thousands of miles, flowing in from the east and the west.

When the canyon was filled with water, there was an immediate swell on the surface of the ocean as the rushing waters collided and bounced back—back toward beaches and coastlines hundreds, even thousands of miles away.

Two swells, one moving west toward the coast of India and the other moving east toward Indonesia, traveled about 500 miles an hour on the open sea. These swells, moving miles above the deep ocean floor, were not readily noticeable, even by ships that were directly in their paths.

The swells turned into waves as they came closer to shore. The water still moving away from shore, and the increasingly shallow ocean floor, slowed the waves to around five or six miles an hour. A wall of water sixty feet high (some say almost one hundred feet high), rushing ashore even at the relatively slow speed of five miles an hour, is capable of horrific, catastrophic destruction.

The northern part of Sumatra, Indonesia, is heavily populated. The city of Banda Aceh spreads out over the western coastline, facing the Indian Ocean. Steep hills rise up on the eastern side of the peninsula, looking over the city and toward the sea.

At the center of this city of 425,000 people is a mosque. Traffic circles the fenced area enclosing the huge white building. The slim white minarets, extending sixty feet or more into the sky, have small windows where the muezzins call out the prayer times to remind Muslims to stop their work, face Mecca, and kneel in prayer. The chants are blared out over loudspeakers in this largely Muslim city whose god is Allah.

Full of the usual markets and stores, the city bustles with traffic. Trucks, delivery vans, sport-utility vehicles, and cars share the road with motorbikes and rickshaws. Although most of the rickshaws are motorized, a few are still foot powered.

The center of the city is less than a mile from the sea. Two- and sometimes three-story buildings are crowded along the streets, filling the entire coastline and even a spit of land joined to the mainland on one end and connected to the city by a bridge at the sea end.

The city swarms with people. Few live out in the country, as Indonesia's political unrest and civil wars keep most away from the highlands.

Fishing has long been a popular, although arduous, way of life for the *Acehnese*. For generations, men and boys have gone to sea, harvesting the fish and bringing home the catch. Their families live in modest homes along the water. Wooden fishing boats—from simple hollowed-out logs to larger, seaworthy vessels equipped with powerful motors and captain's quarters—anchor along the quay. This low-lying area is outlined by dirt levees surrounding cleverly designed fish farms. The seawater covers acres of land, reflecting the hot tropical sun, and fish propagate in the controlled environments.

Some of the people of Banda Aceh have prospered from their enterprises. Natural resources provide means of income, and the fishing industry thrives. The middle class fares quite well in trade and manufacture. Building supplies, home furnishings, electronics, and groceries are readily available. As in many developing countries, cell phones outnumber landline telephones. Schools and higher institutions of learning are scattered throughout the city, and groups of pupils, dressed in their school uniforms, walk to and from classes.

The rich live in multistory, tile-roofed, many-roomed houses. Those of the middle class live in fair-sized concrete block houses, and the poorer people live in rough houses built of wood.

Since this is a Muslim area, most of the women wear dresses and are veiled, although it is not uncommon to see women in Western-style dress with their hair uncovered. The men wear mostly Western-style clothing; however, it is not uncommon to see the more conservative Muslim trousers and tunics. Some men wear the woven hats that specify which tribe they represent.

1

Life Interrupted

Dani dipped water from the tile tank in the bathroom. He poured the cooling water over his head and the water splashed onto the tile floor. As he reached the dipper toward the tank again, he saw the surface of the water erupt into tiny waves. Water suddenly splashed to one side.

Earthquake!

The floor beneath him began to shake. "Earthquake!" he shouted. Small chunks of plaster began raining on his head. He opened the door and called to his wife. "*Aida!* Get the children and go out on the street!"

Grabbing his clothes, he dressed hurriedly. The water was now splashing out of the open tank and the walls of the house were groaning and shaking.

Dashing down the flight of steps that took him to the first floor, Dani heard the screams of his neighbors.

"Come!" Dani called to his two-year-old son, *Sugi*. He ran over to the cot and cried out in horror. Plaster had fallen onto the sleeping boy and covered him in gray dust.

"Papa!" Sugi wailed in terror. Brushing at his face, he tried to sit up.

Grabbing his son, Dani brushed madly at the dust. Tears turned the dust to mud on Sugi's chubby cheeks.

"Dani! Get out!" Their pastor, *Erman*, who had spent the night with their family, yelled from the staircase. "I have Flora with me!" Dani could hear his six-year-old daughter screaming in fear.

The walls were swaying ominously now and Dani could hardly stay on his feet. Books were tumbling off the shelves and the furniture was dancing crazily on the tilting floors.

"Dani," Aida cried to her husband. "Come quickly! The houses are starting to crumble!"

"Do you have the baby?" Dani yelled as he dashed out of the house. Even as he asked, he saw their infant in his wife's arms.

Though the sun was shining brightly and there was no wind, the palm trees that lined the road were shaking violently.

Dani joined his family on the paved road where Aida clung to her children. Erman was praying and holding on to Flora as the ground beneath them rose and fell and shook them sideways. The fences whipped back and forth and huge cracks ran up the outsides of the cement block houses. Roof timbers groaned. Piles of dust rising in the distance indicated that houses were collapsing. Several people who had been standing up were thrown down by the violent shaking.

"Oh, Jesus, help us!" Dani prayed in a desperate voice. Only a recent convert to Christianity, he immediately cried out to God for help.

"Oh, I can't bear to watch!" Aida covered her eyes.

Dani groaned as he saw their house walls begin to crumble and fall. They scooted further away as a billowing cloud of dust rose up from the wreckage. Still, the ground beneath them shook violently.

Harried thoughts ran through Dani's head. The money they had saved from his wages so he could build a house for his young wife and growing family. The years of work he had put into building their house. "Oh, God! Why are you allowing this to happen? What will become of us?"

"Is this the end of the world?" Aida gasped as the ground continued to rock them to and fro.

"I don't know." Dani's voice was hollow as he held Sugi close to his chest and tried to clear the dust out of his young son's eyes.

Erman was praying earnestly. "Dear Lord, forgive all our sins and prepare us to meet you! We come to you in the name of your Son, Jesus Christ!"

Sugi's tears had washed away most of the dust , but his eyes were red and bloodshot. Dani tried to use his shirttail to wipe his son's face clean.

It seemed much longer, but after ten minutes, the shaking slowed, then stopped.

All along the crowded road people began getting to their feet and surveying the damage. Although not nearly all the houses had collapsed, many were damaged. There were shouts and screams from people trapped under the rubble. The entire neighborhood was in chaos.

Cars were crushed beneath timbers. Several houses that had collapsed still had some walls standing. Inside rooms were exposed to public view. Tilting floors hung dangerously over ground floors, and pictures hung crookedly on the walls. A neighbor's porch roof hung down, covering the front door of the house.

After the noise of groaning and protesting buildings died down, only the voices of the people broke the quiet morning. "There will be aftershocks!" someone cried out. "Stay away from the buildings!"

Dani stared at the wreckage of his house. Something deep down inside of him was numb. He felt despair clutch at his heart.

In less than ten minutes, their house was gone. All the work, all the money they had invested—gone.

"At least we have each other," Aida whispered, seeing the despair on her husband's face.

"I know," Dani said slowly. "I wonder how our relatives are."

He looked at his neighbors' houses. There were still many left standing. He looked back at the rubble that was all that was left of their house. Not only their house, but also their shop, their business. His expensive copy machines, photo lab equipment, and all his inventory now lay crushed and ruined under the piles of concrete blocks and twisted timbers.

He got up and walked slowly toward the house. Was there nothing he could salvage? Time seemed to stop. This was all too unreal.

At first, he was barely conscious of a growing swell of voices and a low, ominous sound that came from behind him. The sound was coming from the direction of the sea.

A mob of people was rushing up the road. As they came closer, their cries and screams penetrated his numb mind. Faint cries of "Water! Water!" reached his ears.

Why were the people yelling, "Water! Water!" and running? Even if some of the fishpond dams had broken, there was no danger from them. The city was built on level ground, and it would take a tremendous amount of water to cause flooding.

Yet the screaming and running continued. "Water! Water! Water is coming!"

* * *

Mangasa entered the churchyard, clutching his music sheets under his arm and walking swiftly toward the entrance. There was a tricky part in one song, and he wanted to practice before church services began. A university student, Mangasa had moved to Banda Aceh from an inland city and had become involved in the musical program in the church. He was young and ambitious, dreaming of a future of wealth and influence.

Before he reached the sturdy white church building, he felt a sudden jolt under his feet.

"Whoa!" he exclaimed to himself, hesitating.

There was another tremor, and the ground began to dip and sway beneath him. The palm trees nodded their fronds vigorously and the tall fence surrounding the church began to sway. The tremor increased in violence and there were creaking, groaning noises from all the city buildings around him. He could hear the cries and screams of people fleeing their houses.

Traffic slowed, then stopped as the road buckled beneath the cars and motorbikes. Frantic screams and shrill calls filled the normally quiet Sunday morning air.

Mangasa looked around wildly. He swayed back and forth, trying to keep his footing. At first, he thought he might grab hold of the side of the church house, but as the ground continued to shake and the buildings groaned in protest, he knew he must stay away from any edifice that could collapse. He had felt earthquakes before—enough to realize this one was gigantic.

He sat on the concrete walk leading to the steps and looked up toward the roofline of the church. It was rocking back and forth like a giant ship on the ocean.

Mangasa thought wildly of the church services planned for that day. If the building collapsed, there would be no services. He would not be able to play the organ after all.

Would there be people to come? How many would survive this massive earthquake?

Thoughts darted through his mind like frightened fish. What was his family experiencing?

As the ground continued its crazy tilting and shaking, more sober thoughts came to him.

What if this was the end of the world? He knew the Bible had many prophecies about the last days and earthquakes in different places. Was Jesus coming back right now?

Lifting his eyes, Mangasa gazed heavenward. Was he prepared? Was he ready?

The screaming and crying of people in the streets, the creaking and groaning of buildings, and the heaving and shaking of the ground were unlike anything Mangasa had ever experienced. He glanced at his watch. The digital numbers looked back up at him. 8:08. The seconds continued to blink.

But time seemed to stand still. Was it only ten minutes ago that he had felt the first tremor? How long could the earth shake like this and still hold together? There were no cracks in the ground—just this heaving, shaking, rolling motion of the earth beneath him.

Then, with a final rumble, the earth held still. Mangasa stood up cautiously. He felt dazed.

His cousins! They lived only a few houses from the church. He would go there and see how they had fared. His long legs carried him swiftly out of the churchyard and down the sidewalks. Even as he ran, he took in the damage from the earthquake. Here and there, house walls had collapsed. The sidewalk was littered with debris.

"Mangasa!" he heard his name being called. "Over here!"

It was his cousin. *Edo* was standing arm in arm with his sister, *Nalita*. Their faces were sober and frightened, and Nalita's was streaked with tears.

"Are you all right?" Mangasa asked as he stopped in front of them. "No one is hurt?"

"We got out in time," Edo said soberly.

"Where are your parents?"

Edo shook his head. "They left early this morning to visit our grandparents. I hope they are okay."

Mangasa looked toward the house. It was still standing and, miraculously, hardly showed any damage.

The people around them chattered nervously. The cries of children and the high voices of women were underscored by the lower, tense voices of the men and boys. No one seemed to know what to do next.

When the first faint cries of a mob reached them, they did not know why the people were screaming. Then the first comprehensible cry reached their ears. "Water! Water!"

* * *

Fine lines at the edges of *Sadei's* eyes deepened as he smiled at his two grandchildren. "All ready?" he asked, beaming at the two youngsters as they bounded out of their modest two-story house.

"Yes, dear Grandfather," *Lusi* lilted. She skipped toward the cycle where her grandfather was waiting to take them to church. Her black eyes sparkled and her braids bounced in the early morning sunshine.

"How about you, *Susilo?*"

"I know my memory verses," the ten-year-old boy grinned.

"I am ready."

"Good, good!" Sadei's voice caressed his grandchildren's ears. "This is an important day, just after Christmas. On this Sunday we will continue to celebrate the birth of Jesus!"

Sadei and his family were part of the Christian Chinese fellowship in Banda Aceh. Taking his extended family to church on the cycle was something this elderly man counted a privilege.

Lusi lifted her one leg and prepared to straddle the cycle behind her grandfather. But she was thrown off balance as the cycle jerked away from her.

"Grandfather!" she wailed. "What are you doing?"

Sadei was too busy trying to stay upright to answer her, even though he had both feet firmly planted on the ground. It was not the wavering of the cycle that was upsetting his balance. It was the rising and falling of the ground beneath him.

"Grandfather! What's wrong?" Lusi cried as she jumped away from the wobbling cycle and tried to maintain her balance. She grabbed her brother's arms and the two swayed together.

"Earthquake!" Sadei managed to yell, trying his best to leave his bucking cycle. Just as he dismounted and jumped clear, the cycle fell over. "*Sumiyem!*" His voice strained to call his wife above the noise of the creaking houses all around him.

"Help!" Her cry came from the house.

Trying to stay on his feet, Sadei lurched toward their creaking, groaning home.

"Earthquake! Come out!" Over and over Sadei called, cupping his hands toward the front door.

"Oh! What is happening?" Sumiyem staggered out of the house, trying to stay upright. Her small form was whipped back and forth, yet terror gave her strength to get away from the groaning walls behind her.

"Out to the road! The house might fall on us!" Sadei grabbed his grandchildren's hands, and together the four fought for balance as they moved away from the swaying houses.

"Look, Grandfather! The trees!" Lusi clamped her hand over her mouth in horror as she tried to point to waving palm fronds being shaken violently back and forth. It seemed like a giant, invisible hand was trying to uproot the trees.

"The roof collapsed on *Fifa's* store!" Susilo's head bobbed back and forth as he looked two houses down the street.

The splintering sound of glass bottles mingled with the creaks of straining walls and the cries of people rushing out of their houses. The bottles and groceries in Fifa's market were thrown off the shelves, crashing onto the concrete floor.

"Lord Jesus!" Sadei prayed out loud, "Protect our family!" His eyes took in the damage all around him. "Protect the people in the church! Protect the people of Banda Aceh!" He tightened his grip around his grandchildren's waists as they huddled on the ground.

"I wonder . . ." Sumiyem began, then, glancing at her terrified grandchildren, said no more. Her head was in constant motion as the earth beneath them rocked and heaved. Her eyes looked deep into her husband's and saw her question echoed there.

Sadei caught his wife's gaze. He knew she was thinking of their son, *Ghanda*, and his wife, *Chicha*. But it would not do to worry the children about their parents.

"I want Mama," eight-year-old Lusi whimpered, pressing her face against her grandmother.

"We must pray for their safety!" Sumiyem tried to comfort her granddaughter. Her lips moved as she closed her eyes and swayed back and forth.

For ten more long minutes the earth gyrated and heaved. Grinding moans came from deep inside the earth. Then, thankfully, the ground beneath them was still once more.

A glass bottle fell with a final crash in the market. There was an occasional thump of a concrete block falling from a cracked wall. Voices were hushed for the most part, but subdued cries could be heard rising from seated people as they tried to piece together what had happened.

"Go, Sadei. See if Ghanda's house is standing. See if they are . . . if they are still . . . okay." Sumiyem took a trembling breath and looked imploringly at her husband. "Take the cycle and go!"

"Will you . . . will you and the children be all right?" Sadei asked, his voice trembling, too. "I . . . maybe I should stay here with you. There will be an aftershock."

"No, you must go! We will stay outside." Sumiyem glanced at their still-standing house and pled with her husband. "Go! Go at once to see if they are—if the house is okay."

"Go, Grandfather, please!" Lusi's eyes were swimming in tears and she turned her frightened face up to look into Sadei's eyes.

"I will go," he decided quickly. "Susilo, take care of your sister and grandmother!"

Susilo did not say anything, but nodded soberly.

The road was crowded with people and Sadei had to maneuver his way slowly around the agitated crowds. He saw houses that had collapsed, but not as many as he had feared, for the earthquake had been severe and lasted longer than any other quake he had ever experienced.

He headed west toward his son's house. Toward the ocean.

At first, the crowd of people running toward him made no sense. Why were they rushing toward his part of town? Was there a fire? Had something exploded?

He had to stop. Sadei put one foot on the road to balance his cycle. The road was completely blocked and the crowd was rushing past him. They were saying something. Sadei strained to hear above some great rushing noise that grew louder and louder. A noise coming from the sea.

Then he could hear what the people were crying. "Water! Water!"

What a strange thing to cry at this time! Water! Why were they yelling "water" and running away from the ocean?

* * *

Dani rushed away from his house and peered down the street where the crowd was coming toward him. "Water! Water! A tsunami is coming!"

"What is happening?" Aida screamed at her husband, her baby clutched tightly in her arms.

"The people say water from the ocean is coming," Erman came dashing up to the young family.

"We must run!" Aida screamed, trying to join the fleeing crowd.

"No, no!" Dani yelled, trying to think of a plan. "If it is a tsunami, we cannot outrun it!" Wildly, he looked around.

Making a quick decision, he pulled at Aida's arm. "Come! We will climb up the unfinished building!"

"Look!" Erman yelled. He pointed up the street.

For one brief moment, they stood still, transfixed by the sight.

Power poles were toppling, one after another, being pushed over by a tremendous wave of moving debris. Cars shot up into the air, small boats made a crest, and grinding timbers and tin projected from the moving wall that came rushing down the street.

"Quick!" Dani panicked. "We must run!" Fear shot through them as they ran toward the water, trying to get to the nearby building.

Before they could reach their goal, the wave hit them. Dani gasped as the first wave of oily water swept over his head. Holding tightly to Sugi, he surfaced, ran into the first floor of the building and dashed up the stairs that led to the second floor. Erman was in front of him, carrying Flora.

None too soon. Water gushed into the building and filled it to more than eight feet. Screams of people mingled with the mighty grinding, roaring, groaning sounds of massive amounts of water carrying mountains of debris through the streets.

"Aida! Aida, where are you?" Dani began screaming when he realized his wife was not with them on the second floor. He looked frantically among the people that crowded the second floor. "Aida!"

Erman joined him. "Where is she? She was right in front of me when we got hit!" He put Flora down and went toward the window opening. Dani dashed down the stairs and tried to peer into the murky darkness. "Aida!" His voice trembled in despair. Where was she?

Just outside the window opening downstairs, he saw a form, surrounded by wreckage, struggling to hold onto a bundle. "Aida!" he cried out, and plunged into the oily water, pushing aside floating wood. How he was able to get out the window and reach the side of his wife, Dani never knew.

"Here, give me the baby!" He stood on something solid, and his wife, coughing and choking, clutched him frantically.

"Here! Up here, Dani!" Erman was right above him reaching out for the infant.

Dani handed the crying baby up to his friend. Then he turned back to his wife. "Aida, here, put your weight on this." He pushed a floating timber toward his wife.

Reaching down with his now empty arms, Erman took hold of Aida's hands. "In the name of Jesus, come up!" The words came out strongly. With an upward surge, the woman was out of the still rising water and being pulled through the second floor window opening. Dani clambered up and hoisted himself through the opening.

Aida was sitting on the floor, coughing and spitting out filthy, oily water. Over and over she retched until nothing more came up.

"Here," someone handed them a dry veil, and Dani gently wiped his wife's face.

"Are the children all right?" Aida whispered as soon as he could talk.

"They are all here," Dani reassured her.

"Watch out! Earthquake!" someone shouted from their refuge.

The floor beneath them began to shake.

From somewhere, someone shouted, "Water! Higher water is coming!"

Adrenaline rushing, several of the men somehow managed to punch a hole in the wooden ceiling, and one by one they clambered onto the flat roof. Occasional quakes continued to rock the building. No one knew how long it would be before the building collapsed.

Everywhere Dani looked, he saw destruction beyond belief. At first, he averted his eyes from the corpses floating among the debris. Then shock flooded his mind and numbness settled over him.

"We have to get some of the people off this roof," Erman worried as the crowd of thirty-some people huddled together. "I can feel the timbers sagging beneath us."

Taking charge, he and several other men made a bridge of planks from the roof to the house next door. Dani and his family joined several others working their way toward a three-story building that rose above the roiling waters.

The three adults each carried a child, and Dani made sure Aida was always between him and Erman. They laboriously picked their way over the tile roofs until they reached the taller building.

The large third floor was already crowded, yet no one was turned away. People who had been rescued from the water were lying on the floor, some moaning in pain from cuts and bruises. Almost everyone wore wet, slimy clothes. Faces were hard to recognize, streaked with black oil from the water.

When another earthquake rocked the foundations, almost everyone fled up the narrow stairs to the roof, fully anticipating another wall of water sweeping toward them from the sea.

The concrete roof was flat, and Erman, Dani, and his family sat down on the hot surface. Dani tried to shield the baby from the heat of the sun. Aida leaned weakly against him, the two children huddled in her arms.

The moans and screams of voices in the water were terrible to hear, and the other people on the roof were crying out in fear and anguish.

Erman bowed his head, and Dani could see his lips moving. Then, opening his eyes, he looked at Dani. "Let us pray."

There on the roof, with destruction and death all around them, the three adults joined hands and prayed. "Lord, we believe in your power," Erman prayed, his voice choking with emotion. "We believe you will help us through all of this. You will be the one to save us. Yet, if you choose to take us to heaven, we still believe in you!" His voice faltered, and then, tightening his grip on Dani's hand, he began to sing.

> Oh, Lord my God! When I in awesome wonder
> Consider all the worlds Thy hands have made . . .

Hesitantly at first, Dani and Aida joined in.

How great Thou art, how great Thou art!

Dani's courage grew as he reaffirmed his faith by singing aloud. Something much greater than the circumstances around him made it possible for him to reach out by faith toward God and whisper, "I believe in you!"

Through the recurring quakes from the earth and the horrible sights that washed past them for the next hour, they waited. For what, they knew not.

When the children began to whimper in the heat and ask for water, someone passed them a bottle of water. Even though they were surrounded by strangers, there was a common thread of human decency that bound them together. Later, when the waters had receded, the baser human nature would begin to show itself, and looting, pilfering, and theft would run rampant through the city. For now, everyone was interested in surviving the terrible disaster.

"The water level is falling," Erman said after more than an hour had passed.

They watched the water recede, exposing even more terrible wreckage than before. Cars were upturned and small boats pointed their prows upwards. Wrecked windows and sofas lay about in black heaps. Worst of all were the scores of human corpses that littered the debris. Men, women, and children had been killed. Some bodies were mutilated beyond indentification, even if they had not been covered with black mud. Dani felt sick to his stomach and tried to look away. But he could not escape the gruesome scene. Everywhere he looked, the same sight horrified him.

It was mid-afternoon before the water went down enough that they could peer down onto the street and actually see the road between the piles of debris.

"We must get away from here and find a safe place for the children." Dani told Erman quietly. "If we go toward the mountains, there must be places there that were not flooded."

It was difficult to make any kind of plan. As far as they could see, there was only ruin and destruction. Was there any place that was not damaged? From their vantage point on top of the roof, they looked longingly toward the mountains rising in the distance.

"Let me see if there is a safe way down and then we will try to leave," Erman told his friend.

"Wait! I will go with you. It is better that two go than one by himself." Turning to Aida, he asked, "Will you be all right?"

She nodded and said quietly, "We must find a way out of here."

The two men went down the stairs back onto the third floor. Water had not entered, but it was crowded with people. The air was stifling and it was difficult to breathe.

"You can't go down the stairs," someone told them. "The stairway is blocked by junk."

They headed for an open window and looked out. A house roof had washed up against the second floor and was only inches from the window. They climbed out and worked themselves down alongside the house to the first floor. From here, they could climb down on piles of debris, dodging corpses, until they reached the street.

Familiar landmarks were obliterated. The street was choked with wrecked cars and broken lumber. But they were determined to leave the wrecked area.

Back up by the same route, the two men gathered the children once more in their arms. With Aida, they went slowly down the laborious route across the wreckage. By now, a stream of survivors was slowly working down to the street level. Small groups of people picked their way through the rubbish.

"Here," Erman exclaimed. "Look what I found!" He pulled a package of cookies out of a soggy cardboard box. He showed the plastic-sealed bag to the rest.

The children hungrily ate theirs, but none of the adults could force themselves to eat.

As they picked their way slowly away from the sea, the journey became a continuation of the nightmare that had begun that morning. Broken glass on the road made it dangerous for anyone without shoes, and sharp, jagged metal impeded their progress. Wreckage lay everywhere. They had to detour around overturned cars blocking the road, and more than once they had to clamber over obstacles deposited by the floodwaters. But there was nothing as terrible as the dead bodies. Bodies hung limply from tree limbs, sprawled on rubbish heaps, or lay in masses where the waters had dashed them against walls.

At first, Dani could not help crying when he saw small children lying lifeless beside the road. He hugged Sugi even tighter to his chest and stumbled on, trying to avert his eyes. But the dead were too many. They were everywhere, all around them. Occasionally, he thought he saw a body move, as though there might still be life in it, but he was sure no one could have survived under water all that time.

The small group of survivors continued its horrible journey, trying to get away from the scene of death and destruction all around them.

* * *

"The fishponds must have burst!" Edo exclaimed. "Come, Nalita, let's get the important papers and take them upstairs." The two dashed for the house.

Mangasa could not comprehend what was happening. The crowd of running people confused him. What were they running from?

"Hurry!" he called to his cousins. Something made him want to flee. He felt some disaster was to come.

Then he saw the reason for the people's panic. The moving wall of debris was hurtling down the narrow street toward him.

Wildly calling for his cousins, Mangasa jumped on the cycle and started it. "Edo, you must come! Terrible water is coming!"

The grinding roar of the two-story wave bearing down on him drowned out the screams of the people. At times the wave seemed to stop, then, with an enormous roar, something would give way and the pile of debris would advance again with frightening speed.

Mangasa tried to flee from the monster on the cycle. He had only gone several meters when black oily water was all around him up to his waist. Jumping off the cycle, Mangasa darted into a narrow alley on the heels of a woman and a young girl. The alley was only about three feet wide. A huge coconut tree blocked the other end.

Taking one terrified look behind him, Mangasa saw wreckage block the entrance. The pressure of the wave was so great, water began to fill the alley. They could not exit because of the coconut tree at the other end, and Mangasa felt panic grip his heart.

He joined the two others at the coconut tree, and with a shout of dismay saw black water begin to pour in around the tree. The water swirled around their waists. All three grabbed for the tall, straight trunk of the palm, and as the water rose around them, they kept their heads above water by continuing to climb the trunk. The water rose so rapidly, and things happened so swiftly, that Mangasa scarcely realized when the young girl disappeared. He tried to wipe the scum from his face and desperately clung to the tree. The top of the tree had grown away from the buildings; he was no longer between the two houses, but out over the flooded street. Frantic cries of people hanging onto floating objects reached Mangasa as the floodwaters carried the helpless away.

"I can't hold on any longer!" the woman gasped. Her one hand gripped the tree trunk, and with the other, she reached for Mangasa.

Mangasa held onto her arm. Another wave came and they clambered up the trunk again.

Mangasa's clothes felt heavy, and he had to continually kick with his feet to stay up. When a board crashed up against the tree, he pushed it toward the woman. She rested her upper body on the board and clung tightly to the tree.

Taking a quick look around him, Mangasa saw that all the two-story houses were covered. Only the tops of some of the roof peaks were visible. Three-story houses had shrunk to one-story houses, and boats floated among the wreckage.

"God, is this the end of the world?" Death stared the young man in the face. "What will happen to us?"

Clinging desperately to the tree trunk, Mangasa realized he could drown at any moment. "Lord Jesus, I commit myself into your will. I do not know if I shall live any longer. I want to be ready to meet you!" Desperate cries from his heart rose up over the water-covered city.

"Oh! I cannot hold on much longer." The woman moaned in distress. "Daddy! Daddy, where are you?" She tried to shout but was able only to moan.

The water began to recede. Mangasa, gripping the trunk with his legs, inched down the tree. The rooftops became larger, and he saw they were only about nine feet from the edge of the nearest roof. "Come!" he told the woman. "Let's swim to the roof top!"

The woman draped herself across the board as Mangasa pushed her ahead of him until they reached the rooftop. They clambered up the hot tile roof and sat on the ridge.

In the distance, Mangasa saw a few other people sitting on rooftops. He could see movement inside the windows of the three-story buildings. But he knew the survivors were in the minority, for the thousands in the city could not all have found refuge. He looked at the woman. Her face was beaded with sweat, and she stared out across the water that lapped at the sides of the houses. She did not speak.

The sun continued to smite them with intense heat. Mangasa drew his shirt up over his head to try to shield himself. His mouth felt dry and he longed for a drink of water.

As the hours dragged by, Mangasa's thoughts were busy. His mind went back to his cousins. Where were they? What about all the people who had been planning to come to church that day? How many of them had survived?

He looked toward where the ocean usually was. Now the ocean was all around him, and it was hard to get his bearings.

The part of the city that had been built right along the coast must have been completely covered. If the water had risen more than two stories here on the slightly higher ground, then the lower areas must be completely destroyed.

Why had the water risen? It must have been a result of the earthquake. Some massive upheaval on the ocean floor must have pushed the water out over the land.

But something more personal was going on inside his heart. Eternity loomed ahead of him. What if another, even greater wave came and swept him away? It seemed quite possible, as the house roof trembled and tilted beneath him with each subsequent quake of the earth.

"God, I am sorry for all the selfish ambitions that I have had. You know I wanted to be a rich and famous person. I see that all that is worth nothing when the time comes to die. Forgive me and help me to live only for you!"

On the hot rooftop, Mangasa knew only one thing mattered. "I put all my trust in you, Jesus. I thank you for revealing yourself to me through this terrible experience. I want to live only for you! That is all that matters."

He shifted and tried to protect his arms from the burning sun. He looked at the water level. Was it receding? Was the water going back out to the ocean where it belonged?

He heard the woman beside him moan. He looked at her. Her head was bowed and he saw the sun beat unmercifully on her. He took his shirt and covered her head. The woman did not look up.

* * *

Sadei sat motionless on his cycle, trying to take it all in. Whatever was wrong with the people, all crying, "Water!" and running towards him? There was no way he could continue—the street was full of rushing figures.

Turning his cycle, Sadei decided to try another street. He tried to see what was behind the crowd, but still could not see anything. Just screaming, frightened people.

Then, looking down at his feet, he saw the first small wave of water lapping against his legs. There really was water! Sadei felt extremely puzzled.

Then, a scream of horror made him look beyond the crowd, and a nightmarish sight met his eyes.

A black wall of water was carrying cars as though they were toys, tossing them up into the air and turning them in crazy circles. Sadei gunned the cycle and raced away from the menace behind him. There was no time to try to think what was happening. All he could think was that he must get back to his house and try to rescue his family.

Water swirled all around him when he reached their house. He jumped from the cycle and ran toward the front door.

With a roar, the wave engulfed him, spinning him around and around. He felt himself being banged up against something hard and instinctively grabbed for it. He found himself grasping metal bars. Debris jammed up against him and oily water submerged him over and over again. Still, Sadei held onto the bars.

Gasping for breath, the aged man was buffeted by the wave. Over and over again his lungs cried out for air, and his body was tortured as wood hit him with tremendous force.

Sadei's hands trembled and more than once he thought he was losing consciousness. He could pray no words. In his conscious thoughts he could only cry, "Lord Jesus, have mercy! Save my soul!"

Time stood still. Everything in Sadei fought for survival, battling against the watery monster that was overpowering him and tossing him about like a helpless toy.

Then, there was a lull. The water no longer surged against him, and Sadei's mind cleared. He looked around him.

He had been gripping the bars of the tall gates guarding the courtyard of the houses in his compound. He was at the very top of the gates against the third floor ceiling of the buildings. His feet were resting on wreckage piled up two stories beneath him.

It did not make sense to Sadei. How had he ever gotten to the very top? He did not remember climbing up the bars. The water must have picked him up and shoved him against the high gates, and he had just clung tightly to the bars.

He could tell the water was receding. All around him rooftops began appearing. He could see several figures huddled together on top of the roofs in the blazing sun.

Sadei loosened his grip on the bars and sat down on the edge of a timber that was fairly horizontal. His arms and legs trembled violently. He tried to wipe the sludge off his face with his sleeve.

The piles of trash all around him were a chilling combination of house roofs, timbers, doors, windows, furniture, and broken timbers. Yet more chilling were the silent figures of drowned people, all mixed into the debris. Sadei groaned and tears made clean furrows down his wrinkled cheeks.

Where were Sumiyem and the grandchildren? What had happened to them?

He was only one house away from his own home. Carefully, avoiding the sharp metal, he picked his way over the wreckage. He became aware of his own injuries as he climbed over the mounds toward his house.

"Sumiyem!" he called anxiously as he clambered up the pile of junk that had washed up against his house. He reached the second floor window and looked inside. He saw some people moving around. Was his family inside?

He climbed through the window. "Sumiyem!" He recognized several of his neighbors.

"She is not here!" a neighbor lady shook her head. "We took refuge here but we have not seen your family. My husband . . ." her voice trailed away and she buried her face in her hands.

"Susilo? Lusi?" His voice sounded hoarse.

Negative headshakes sent his heart plummeting. Where could they be? He wandered about, peering out the windows. Everything was soaked with water and ruined.

The earth shook beneath them again and the walls swayed. Was there no end to this nightmare? For some reason, Sadei felt as though nothing mattered anymore. Where was his family? Oh, he should have stayed with them!

"Water! Water!" the cry came from outside. With a cry of alarm, Sadei and the few neighbors raced up the narrow steps onto the flat concrete roof.

But the water level did not rise. Or, if it did, it did not make much difference this time. The ocean was already all around them. How was it possible to do more damage? The city already lay destroyed all around them as far as they could see. It was no longer a city, but a cemetery. A cemetery with unburied bodies.

Sadei felt weak. He sat on the concrete roof and bowed his head. A sense of helplessness swept over him. Where was the rest of his family? Where were his sons? The children's parents? His relatives? Was he the only survivor?

Mercifully, clouds covered the sun and gave some protection from the heat. But it no longer seemed to matter.

"You are the only hope I have," he prayed. "Help me to keep my faith in you, Lord."

"Papa," a voice called from below. "Papa!"

It was *Sutomo*, his youngest son! "Here I am, Son." Sadei went to the edge of the roof and peered down.

"Are you okay?" Sutomo called out anxiously. "Where are Mama and the children?"

"Go look for them," Sadei told him. "They are not here. No one knows where they are."

"Oh, Papa! I thought everyone must have died. I . . . " his voice trailed away as he dashed his fists against his eyes. "I was in town when the water hit, and I somehow managed to get on top of a roof and then later went to the mosque. The water is not so high in the middle of town. Water only in the first floors."

"Son, go look for Mama and the children. Maybe they need help." Sadei nodded his head in encouragement.

He watched his sixteen-year-old son turn and pick his way through the rubble. Every step was treacherous.

* * *

For Dani and his family, the days following the tsunami were filled with uncertainties. They learned the magnitude of the destruction along the coast of Indonesia and other coastal areas. Dani realized that though he lost his house and all his equipment, his story is an amazing one simply because no one in his immediate family was lost. As he recounted his experiences with other people, that fact stood out sharply, because most survivors lost part—often all—of their families.

"In the days that followed the tsunami, I struggled a lot with why a loving God would allow this calamity to happen," Dani said when

he had told me his story. "Even though we were able to stay with friends who also ran a photo shop, our life seemed to come to an end.

"It became very difficult to find food for our children and ourselves, as so many people were in need. The health situation became unbearable with the decaying bodies all around us, and we left for the capital city, Medan. We stayed there for six months, then finally came back here to our city.

"There are still many times that I wake from horrible nightmares. I don't trust the ground beneath my feet anymore, and were it not for the encouragement from people at church, I would have even more difficulty keeping my faith.

"I don't know what will become of my family. We are now renting a house and I want to begin a photo shop again to provide an income for us, but it will be very difficult. I am still a young man, but my business has been swept away and I do not see how I can begin again. It took us nine years to build our shop and house, and it cost us around one hundred thousand U.S. dollars to build it. Now, it is all gone."

Later, Dani's pastor friend, Erman, told me that many times Dani seems to become fainthearted and discouraged. It has definitely affected his Christian faith, and Erman is praying that somehow Dani can reach out by faith and feel the love of God in his distress.

Erman himself is single, and yet he has a tremendous job to do. Out of their congregation of several hundred people, many have lost family members. He is constantly counseling, encouraging, and trying to help however he can. The building where they held services was destroyed, and they are renting the third floor of another building. There is not enough room.

The situation looks hopeless, yet the Sunday I attended the church with Dani and his family, there was a spirit of worship and praise among these Christians of Banda Aceh, and many stood in the back to join the Sunday service.

* * *

"I want to introduce to you a survivor of the tsunami in Banda Aceh," the moderator motioned his hand toward Mangasa. "He will share his testimony."

Mangasa walked to the podium and faced the audience. The sea of faces looked expectantly at him.

"My name is Mangasa, and it is now a little more than six months since the tsunami devastated the seacoasts around us," he began.

"But I will not tell you about the catastrophe. I will tell you about what happened to me personally."

In clear, simple language, Mangasa painted a word picture of his experience hanging onto the coconut tree. "I did not think of cars, fancy houses, or anything money can buy. I thought of one thing. I thought of God." His voice faltered, then he continued. "All the time I sat on that house roof, waiting for the water level to go down, my mind was busy. I repented from any sin I could think of. The sins I had committed, and perhaps even more noteworthy, the sins I had thought of committing. I repented of all of them. Why? Because death stared at me and I wanted to come to God with a clean heart.

"After I helped the lady off the roof onto a pile of wreckage and we got back down on street level, God spoke some more to me. It was terrible seeing all the dead people around me. The wreckage of cars, houses, and personal possessions was terrible, yet nothing was as terrible as seeing how many hundreds, even thousands, of people had died.

"The flood was no respecter of people. Old people, middle-aged people, young people, children and babies—all lay silent in death.

"I saw the poor people, lying still. They had died poor. I saw the rich with what had been expensive clothes, all drenched and dirty with the oily water, dead. Their expensive jewelry had not saved them. Their position in the city had not helped them. They died just like anyone else.

"God impressed a great truth on me. Even though there are rich and poor, old and young, common and famous people, all will die. Thousands died in the flood. But all of the millions who survived the flood, or were not even touched by the tsunami—these, too, must die someday.

"Again, there is only one thing that matters. Is Jesus Christ the Saviour of my soul? Am I ready to die?" Mangasa paused and looked soberly over the crowd.

"In the days that followed, people were trying to leave the city. There was much confusion as the living looked for their relatives. Many of us never found the bodies of our relatives. We never heard what happened to Edo and Nalita, never found their bodies." Tears seeped out of the corners of Mangasa's eyes and he swallowed hard.

"I have had people tell me, 'Oh, God saved you from the flood because you are a good person!'

"I say to everyone, God has not saved me because of good deeds I have done. God saved me for a reason. I want to live out that purpose by giving myself completely to the will of God for my life. Whatever that is, that is what I want to do. The purpose and focus for my life have been changed by the tsunami."

Mangasa left the podium and returned to his seat.

That evening, when the pastor extended a call for repentance, the Spirit moved among the people, and many repented.

Today, Mangasa is back in Banda Aceh and is a Sunday school teacher in his church. He is an assistant to the pastor, both in the church and in the pastor's business of helping people rebuild small businesses.

"We found the body of my wife the next day," Sadei told me. "We immediately had a small funeral, for the situation was becoming desperate with all the decaying bodies.

"We never found the bodies of my son, his wife, and the two children, Susilo and Lusi," Sadei said, tears running down his face. "I don't know which was worse; not finding their bodies and having our hopes slowly die away as time went on, or finding the body of my wife."

I waited as Sadei struggled to gain his composure.

"We were airlifted to Medan and there I was taken to the hospital. I had some difficulties from the polluted water I had

swallowed and needed treatment for the cuts and bruises I had on my body.

"Now we must go on. I have my youngest son with me and we live with friends whose house was not destroyed.

"The biggest help has been our Christian church. Our pastor has provided special counseling to help us cope with our losses. We all lost someone in our family or extended family. When we came back from Medan after several months, every evening we went to the church for prayer and fellowship. I gathered so much strength from my Christian friends."

At the end of the interview, Sadei said, "I was raised as a Buddhist, but when I was an adult, I heard the story of Jesus. I made the choice to convert to Christianity and tried to raise my family for God. Now, how thankful I am that, during the earthquake and the tsunami, I had the Lord to turn to. He is my comfort."

2

Water Is Coming!

As she had countless Sundays before, *Atika* sat at the small table in her kitchen, drinking her morning coffee. Her husband, *Senno*, was taking a bath, and their two grown children, Micah, almost thirty, and *Yunita*, twenty-two, were somewhere in the house, preparing for church.

The first tremor rattled the dishes in the cupboard and splashed the coffee out of Atika's cup onto the table. As the floor beneath her tilted, Atika screamed and rose from her chair.

"Earthquake!" Her cry was echoed by Micah's bass voice from his room. "Quick, we must get out!"

Since the family lived above their auto parts store, they immediately headed for the stairs.

"Senno, come! Earthquake!" Atika screamed. She knew her husband must have already realized what was happening, as the walls of their house were creaking and swaying with the movements of the earth. But she felt as though she needed to warn him, to make contact with him.

"I'm coming!" Senno yelled, even as the door opened. With his shirt still open, he grabbed Atika's arm. They hurried down the stairs together, bracing themselves against the walls of the staircase as the steps beneath them swayed and creaked.

"Mama! Papa!" Yunita yelled, fear pitching her voice into a shrill screech. "Come, get out! Now!"

"We're coming," Senno yelled, dodging the auto parts falling from the shelves onto the floor.

Staggering, the couple held onto each other as they crossed the sidewalk outside the front door and joined their children.

The road heaved beneath them. Small cracks ran across the blacktop as the earth rose up.

"I can't stand up!" Atika screamed as a strong quake sent them reeling.

"Sit down, Mama," Micah yelled, squatting on his haunches. He steadied himself by placing his hands on the road beside him.

The screams of their neighbors mingled with the groans of the houses, built side-by-side up and down the road. Holding onto each other, the people tried to sit upright, but intermittent, violent shakes caused a new outcry as they were tossed up and down like pieces of driftwood.

Minutes dragged by. There was no let-up, no lull in the massive shaking beneath them. Houses swayed back and forth as the earth rose and fell beneath them. Parked cars shifted one way and then the other. Cycles had fallen over and sprawled on the ground in awkward positions. And still the earth shook in massive movements.

"Oh, Lord," Senno prayed, "be with us during this terrible time. Deliver us from this terrible experience."

"It must be the end of time!" Atika cried in fear. She desperately wanted to grasp something stable.

"We must all pray," Senno said firmly. "This is the time to turn to our faith in Jesus Christ."

Together, the family prayed. Atika could only say, "Lord, have mercy on us. Save us! Lord, have mercy on us!" She clung to the words, trying to shut out the scene around her.

The earth finally quieted. The road no longer heaved beneath them. Cautiously Atika got to her feet, helped up by Senno. They stood, straddle-legged, ready if the ground should begin shaking again.

"Our house is still standing," Senno said thankfully.

"We will have to repair that upper wall," Micah said, pointing to a wide crack running from the top of the second floor window to the eaves.

"Look at the mess in the shop," Yunita said, peering in the front door.

They all went inside. The floor was covered with auto parts, and most of the shelves along the wall were bare. Glass bottles were broken, and greasy liquids seeped underneath the rubble in black puddles.

"Everything looks fairly good up here," Senno called down from the second floor. "The ceilings have cracks, but they are not damaged greatly." Relief flooded his voice.

"I'm going to move the car out of the garage," Micah said, heading for the door.

"Yes, there might be an aftershock," Atika assented. "The car will be safer outside."

"Everyone, come with me," Micah said uneasily, looking around at the junk lying on the floor of their shop.

"Why?" Yunita asked quickly, her dark eyes staring at her brother.

"I just think . . . we might be safer . . . we should leave here." His sentences jumbled together.

"Take the car out first," Senno called from upstairs.

Micah left and Atika picked up a car ramp in front of her and leaned it against the wall.

"Will there be church today?" Yunita asked.

"I don't know," Atika said. "I forgot all about what day of the week it is."

They could hear the car stop in the street in front of the house. The door slammed and Micah stood in the doorway. "Come! I think we should leave this place."

"Where would we go?" Senno, who had come downstairs, asked his son.

Micah looked down at the floor. "I don't know. I just have this feeling that we need to leave."

For a moment no one said anything.

"Well, we need to wash up first," Atika said, looking at her grimy hands.

"All right," Senno decided. "We will go to the church and see if there will be services. I'm guessing the baptism will be canceled for today."

They all went upstairs and Atika sat down in the living room. Suddenly she felt drained.

Yunita straightened the pictures on the walls and picked up broken glass from a shattered flower vase.

Atika heard Micah leave the shop again. She got up and looked out the window, down to the street. All up and down the street, people were assessing the damage. Several cycles puttered up the street and a car slowly drove past. In the distance, she saw several hurrying figures, running toward their houses.

Atika turned and looked into the kitchen. What a mess! Broken dishes and overturned canisters littered the floor.

She heard Micah's voice outside the window, just below the kitchen. There was a sharp note in his query.

Then came the sound of running feet. Atika headed toward the window to look out.

"Mama, Papa! Come quickly! People are running down the street."

It was true. More and more people were running toward the center of the city, away from the sea.

"What is it?" Micah yelled at a teenaged boy running past their house. The boy did not answer, but ran wildly on.

"*Paristo!*" Micah called out to a man he recognized. "What is happening? Why is everybody running?"

Not even pausing in his jog, Paristo yelled, "Water is coming!" He broke into a run.

"You must all come," Micah's voice rose in panic. He was darting up the stairs. "People are saying water is coming. Hurry, Papa! Get in the car. We must leave!"

Atika started for the stairs. She could hear Yunita's frightened cries, "Hurry, Papa!"

"Mama!" Micah's voice was high-pitched. "Where are you?"

"Coming," Atika answered, going down the familiar stairs.

A dull roar in the distance bewildered Atika. What was that noise? In spite of the cries and screams of voices outside the house, she could hear a menacing roar, growing louder and louder.

The screams outside grew shriller. "Run, run! Water is coming! Run, run!"

It was the panic she heard in the voices that made Atika dart toward the front door. "Water is coming!" That made no sense, and yet some horrible danger was threatening them all.

"Papa, get into the car. Now!" Micah's voice was screaming beside her now and Yunita was crying loudly, "Mama! Oh, Mama!"

"I must help Mama," Senno insisted, turning toward his wife. "Come quickly!" He reached out his hand toward Atika.

All around them the screams of the running crowd, now filling the street, were yelling one thing. "Water! Water is coming!"

"Help!" Atika yelled shrilly. "Oh, Senno!" She lunged for her husband's outstretched hand as a wall of water washed over her.

Something heavy knocked Atika over. She fell with a scream, grabbing Micah's hand with a desperate grip. Nasty water washed over her.

For one brief moment, she surfaced. Her eyes were wide with fright as she saw a boat come sailing toward her. Then, hitting something solid, the wooden craft veered to the left. This slowed the deluge for only a moment, then another wave bore down on her.

Micah was still beside her. "Where is Papa?" He gave one wild cry, and they were covered with water again.

Atika felt sure they were going to die. Her mind cried out, "Lord Jesus, save us!" There was nothing else, no one else, she could turn to at a time like this.

Then she felt a smooth surface underneath her arms. Her head surfaced again.

"Mama, grab hold of the door," Micah yelled, helping his mother inch her way onto the floating door.

With a surge of adrenaline, Atika pulled herself up higher on the floating door. Micah struggled to keep it from slipping sideways.

Dirty water lapped around them in disgusting waves.

"Over here!" people were calling to them from a third-story window. Micah kicked against the debris and propelled them toward the cries.

"Yunita!" Suddenly, there she was, hanging on to the coconut tree, right beside them. "Where is Papa?" Atika gasped.

Yunita shook her head. Her face was barely recognizable as she struggled to clean the oily water from her eyes.

The three cautiously worked toward the tall building. Lumber from houses floated all around them, and they had to maneuver around partially submerged cars.

When they finally reached the building, they realized they were still at least three feet below the sill. "Drop a rope or something down!" Micah yelled.

"We don't have a rope," a man's voice called. "Oh, here, use this." He let down one end of a piece of fabric.

"Mama, you go first," Yunita urged.

"No, no! You must go first! We will push from below." Standing on the wreckage, Micah and Atika helped the young girl up. Then Atika was pulled up, and finally Micah came up hand over hand.

Using the fabric to clean their faces, the three sat on the floor. Another quake shook the building, and the people cried out in fear. Atika tried to still her racing heart. She felt completely drained.

"Where is your papa?" she asked again, her voice breaking. "Oh, what has happened to him?" She began to sob quietly.

"He was right beside us," Micah said soberly. "Then the water hit us and I did not see him again."

"Maybe he was washed somewhere else," Atika decided, clinging to any hope she could think of. "Perhaps he is on a roof somewhere."

In her desperation, Atika turned to God. "Let us pray. Only God can help him. And us!" The three bowed their heads in prayer.

As the earth rocked beneath them, the house no longer seemed any safer than the wreckage outside. The walls creaked and groaned. It would have been no surprise if the ceiling had suddenly collapsed.

"We will stay right here by the window," Micah decided. "If the house begins to collapse, we can jump out the window. But whatever happens, we must stay together. We cannot be separated from each other."

After the quake stopped, there was nothing else to do but wait. Even after the water level went down, no one really knew what to do next. Any food or water that had been in the house had long been consumed.

Finally, in the late afternoon, Micah said, "We must leave. There is no food here, and we cannot take refuge here overnight."

Atika agreed. "Perhaps we can find Senno." Her mind wanted to block out the thought that he might have drowned. Even when reason tried to convince her that her husband was gone, she clung desperately to hope. Hadn't the three of them miraculously survived? Surely there was hope that Senno was still alive too.

Yet after they had gone down the stairs and worked their way out onto the street, Atika found herself looking at every body lying in the rubble. Sometimes it was difficult to see if the dead person was a man or a woman. Clothes had been torn off and all the corpses were covered with slime. At first, they all looked the same—gray and lifeless, sprawled in the mud.

"No, no," Atika found herself moaning over and over again as she looked for some recognizable sign among the dead.

"Mama, come!" Yunita begged. "We must get to the city!"

Atika could not help it. Every time she saw another dead body, she had to look closely to see if it was Senno. This took a long time, for the dead lay everywhere. She did not look long at the quiet forms of children. She was looking for the adult form of her husband. How could she go on living without him?

They went past where their house had been. No walls were standing, just a collapsed roof on top of rubble. Micah led them on.

Atika felt faint. They had not eaten since that morning and her throat was dry from thirst. She stumbled on, tears blinding her sight so that she had to use the edge of her sleeve to brush her face. She knew she looked awful, her clothes wet and filthy, but she did not care. Her entire being was crying out for her husband, and the drowned city seemed but an echo of how she felt inside.

"Here, Mama," Micah said, "Eat some of these cookies to give you strength." He had found the cellophane-wrapped package among the debris. The package had kept the cookies completely dry and clean.

The cookies were tasteless to Atika. She ate, knowing she needed the strength from the food, but her thirst increased.

Their journey was taking them into a different area. The ground was higher here and the tsunami had not been as devastating. Water had flooded the first floors of the houses and shops, but most of the buildings were still standing.

"Do you have any water?" Micah called out to a man inside a small food shop.

"Yes, come!" The man beckoned to them and handed them three bottles of water.

"Thank you! God bless you!" Atika said before she drank deeply. Tears pricked her eyelids at the kindness of the stranger.

"The church! I can see the roof of the church," Micah encouraged them after they had been walking for an hour. Normally, it would not have taken that long to walk to the church building, but they had to go slowly through the wreckage-filled streets.

And besides, Atika could not help looking at the corpses along the way, hoping to find her husband. Sense told her his body would not be this far away, yet she could not stop looking for him.

The big white church was a welcome haven for the three, not only for the shelter, but also for the fellowship with the other survivors from their church. The pastor was there, praying and comforting the weeping ones. Everyone had a story of grief and loss. Atika began to realize how enormous the calamity was. Her loss was echoed over and over by the people from the city.

* * *

Purnama reflected on the huge gathering that had finally gotten some of his Buddhist friends into church. Occasionally he had gotten a few men from the large Buddhist community to come to services, but not until the day before, on Christmas Day, had so many showed up. More than thirty had come.

They came yesterday to be a part of the worship service and to hear the story of the birth of Jesus Christ. As Purnama had hoped, they stayed for the festive meal afterward. There they were able to talk firsthand with the Christians and ask any questions they wanted.

He roused himself from his thoughts. There was no time to waste. The sun was already shining warmly through the open window, and he still wanted to get some things ready for the worship service today.

"Make them keep their promises," he prayed under his breath. Yes, the Buddhists had promised they would come back today, but Purnama knew that it would take more than just promises to bring them back. "I pray that somehow the Spirit's touch on some hearts yesterday would create such a great longing to know Jesus that they'll come back. I leave that all in your care!"

There was a reason that Purnama had such a burden for the Buddhist community in Banda Aceh. An only son, Purnama had been raised to take responsibility as the head of the family. This meant not only making domestic and financial decisions, but also carrying on the religious traditions carefully taught to him.

When he was only ten, Purnama had attended a church with some of his childhood friends. There he heard about Jesus, the God of the Western world, as he thought of Him at that time. His parents did not mind that he attended church with his friends. They were open-minded, they thought, and wanted their only son to explore other religions too.

What they did not realize was the deep hunger that developed in Purnama's soul. He felt frustrated with his life and did not find any answers from the stony-faced god to whom he prayed and made sacrifices. Instead, his troubled mind sought comfort from the messages he heard at the Christian church.

After his conversion, Purnama's father reacted in horror. Especially when he, as a teenager, refused to join him in the ancestral worship that all practicing Buddhists participate in. "You want your mother to have to go hungry?" his father scolded. He was scandalized that his son would not pray for his deceased mother. "You yourself will have to eat grass after you die. Your children will not pray for you, and after I die, there will be no one left to pray for us!"

Time and time again, Purnama tried in vain to explain to his father what Jesus now meant to him, but his father was bitterly opposed to his sixteen-year-old son being baptized in the Christian church. But so strong was Purnama's desire to follow Christ that he endured the shame heaped upon him by his father and extended family.

Several years later, Purnama moved and became a part of a Christian church in Banda Aceh. He was barely twenty when the church asked him to be an assistant pastor. Only a few years later, he was ordained.

"I must hurry and take my bath and get to church." Again Purnama forced his mind to return to the present. "Thank you, Jesus, for revealing yourself to me. Thank you for all you have done."

"Joy to the world, the Lord is come." His voice filled the bathroom. With anticipation, he looked forward to the service.

Now thirty years old, Purnama had never married. Living in the upstairs of the church building, he did not have time to feel lonely. Church work kept his days occupied, and he tirelessly used his energy to serve the people. Yesterday, more than three hundred people had crowded into the church building. He hoped for more today.

He felt the floor beneath him tilt. "Hmm, another earthquake," Purnama said to himself. He continued washing himself.

Another tremor shook the entire building and Purnama slid toward the wall. "Ahh! A big one this time."

He heard the calls of the workers who had gathered early to make preparations for the service. "Run! Earthquake!"

When the ceiling cracked open above him, Purnama did not waste any time. He grabbed his towel and dashed out the door. Barefooted, he dashed down the stairs and out into the street. The entire church house was moving back and forth as he stumbled away.

"Is everyone out?" he called to the workers as he joined them. He was thrown down onto the road when an especially severe jolt sent him flying.

"I'm scared!" ten-year-old *Cahya* whimpered.

"Come here," Purnama invited, stretching out his arms to the bewildered boy. "We will pray and ask God to protect us."

Cahya, the son of church workers, crawled into Purnama's lap. He hid his head against the pastor's chest.

"There goes the fabric shop house!" someone yelled. The cries of people on the street grew in crescendo as the cement building collapsed in a cloud of dust.

"I am surprised more buildings are not collapsing," one of the men said in an awed tone as they all watched the ground rise and fall beneath the buildings, built side by side facing the street.

Then, and no one would have thought it possible, the ground heaved even more rapidly, as moaning sounds came from deep within the earth.

People began crying out in fear, clutching at the road in anguish.

Purnama groaned, "It is the end of time, surely. Oh, please God, save us! Help us endure this awful time. Even so, come, Lord Jesus!"

All around him, he could hear people praying. Cries were ascending to Allah, to Buddha, and, from their small group, to the living Lord Jesus Christ.

Purnama looked upward. He was so convinced that the last day had finally come that he searched the bright sky for the falling stars he knew would accompany the end of time. He was bewildered when no bright lights appeared.

However, it was difficult to really think straight. There was too much happening, too many needs right around him to think long on one subject. All he could do was pray.

The minutes went on and on. Finally, like a miracle, the earth stopped rumbling and shaking. Cautiously the people got up from the road and began to assess the damage.

Purnama had gone inside to finish getting dressed and had just stepped outside again when the news came sweeping along the street. One of the casualties of the earthquake was the huge, modern supermarket that had opened several years ago. A wonderful sign of affluence for their city was now in ruins. People were telling each other what buildings had collapsed, and news spread quickly by the myriad of cell phones.

As he finished buttoning his shirt, Purnama told a worker, "I will take the cycle and see what damage has been done to the city." He jumped on the cycle and left to go toward the center of the city.

He had barely gone a quarter of a mile before he saw a sight that burned itself in his memory. Coming down the street toward him was a crowd of people. A wall of waterborne debris, as high as the two-story buildings, was chasing the fleeing crowd. Purnama stopped the cycle, and for a moment was frozen immobile at the incomprehensible sight.

Water? He heard the screams of the crowd. It did not look like water, but like a solid wave of cars, tin, and timbers being forced toward him with enormous pressure. A solid wave, yet strangely liquid. Spouts of water gushed out through the wave of debris.

Purnama tried to turn his cycle, but the wave was too swift. He had barely begun to speed away when the water reached him.

With a wild leap, Purnama left his drowning cycle and clasped his arms around a coconut palm. He tried to climb up the pole-like trunk as dirty water swirled around his legs.

Four other people were clinging to the tree as well. Purnama looked back down at his cycle in time to see two women grab at the handlebars, only to tumble over as the force of the wave hit them. He shuddered in horror as he saw them disappear beneath the debris and the filthy water.

He had to climb higher! Water was rushing toward him from two sides. Purnama could not begin to comprehend what was happening. Where was the water coming from? Why was there water here in the city? Obviously, the sea had spilled out over the shore and was now in possession of the land.

But there was no time to think. Chunks of wood were hitting his legs. In a desperate attempt to escape the cascade of debris, he climbed up higher on the tree. His fingers strained to keep his grip. A car came crunching past him and he swung his right leg away to keep from being ground by the bumper. The cries of the others who had been clinging to the palm diminished, and Purnama saw two of them being swept away by the deluge. With labored breathing, he tried to work himself even higher. Oily water swirled around him, then suddenly he was up to his shoulders in water.

"Oh, God, please save me! If I die, take me straight home to you." The black water surged over his head and tore him from the trunk as it knocked over the tree. The force of the wave tore at his body. He felt himself tumble through the wreckage, his body battered and scoured by the debris.

When his lungs were crying out for air, something forced Purnama's head up out of the water. He gasped for breath. Above him were the rafters of a house stripped of its metal roofing. Around him roiled the water and the wreckage. Then another wave surged toward him, and once more Purnama was submerged.

"Receive me into your kingdom." Even in this chaotic situation, something deep inside his heart knew whom to cry to. "Forgive all my sins and take me to you."

He was pushed up against a steel cable and instinctively grabbed at it. He struggled upward and surfaced, gasping for air. Sputtering and spitting out the turgid water, Purnama tried to take deep breaths.

With his remaining strength, he clung desperately to the cable. He did not let go when another wave pushed him up against a concrete wall. The top of the wall was barely above the water, but Purnama grabbed at it and pulled his weakened body up on the narrow surface. He lay there, panting for breath and trying to cough up the water he had swallowed. Almost in a stupor, he lay face down, gripping the sides of the wall.

His thoughts ran wildly. If the water continued to rise, he would be swept away. There was nothing he could do about it. Debris pounded against the side of the wall, and he felt the concrete shudder beneath him as quakes continued to shake the earth.

Yes, it must be the end times! Never in his wildest imaginations had he thought he would experience anything like this. Why had the Christians not been taken up before this calamity? Nothing made sense.

"God, I don't know what is happening. Yet I turn to you, for there is no one else to turn to. No one but you! Please, whatever you want,

I want that too. Just take me home to be with you in heaven." He felt tears course down his cheeks.

"Why are you punishing us? What have we been doing wrong? What about my family who does not believe in Jesus? Where are the people from the church? What is happening to us?" Questions flowed through his mind in an endless procession.

For a long time, Purnama lay there, trying to piece together some reasonable explanation for what was happening. The earthquake must have triggered an enormous tsunami. But never before had the sea risen like this. Not this high!

"Seawater rising! Water is coming higher!" Purnama heard someone shout from close by.

When his strength returned, Purnama raised his head from the hard concrete and looked around him. Just a short distance away, he saw the rooftop of a government building slanting upward, its red roof tiles looking solid and safe.

Slowly he raised himself up and walked along the wall until he could jump onto the roof. The hot tile roof was not steep, so he easily went up to the ridge.

Two men sat on the ridge, staring out toward the sea. A wave came toward them, pushing fishing boats into the city. All around them, rooftops poked up out of the water. On a few roofs Purnama could see people sitting on the ridgelines.

The wave hit the building they were on and deposited debris on the tiles. But the wave was not high enough to reach them.

"They are all gone," one of the men said, groaning. "The last I saw them, they were running down the street. I tried to get to them, but the water just hit them and they were gone." His voice was low-pitched and his eyes stared at the water. "All gone," he repeated.

The other man said nothing. He sat and looked out over the muddy water and kept turning around and around and looking in all directions. His eyes were glazed, and Purnama wondered what calamity he had experienced. But he did not ask. He felt too emotionally drained himself. He noticed a cut on the man's foot. It was oozing blood, but there was nothing Purnama could do to help.

The amazing thing to him was that he himself was not injured. He had bruises, but there were no open cuts anywhere on his body. Even his bare feet were unscathed, except for a small scratch on top of his right foot. The scratch was so tiny it hardly showed.

"Thank you, God," he breathed in awe. "You protected me from any serious injury!"

What time was it? So much had happened so fast that Purnama had lost all track of time. It must be only mid-morning. Had an hour passed since the first wave had hit? Had it been two hours ago that he had lain on top of the concrete wall? In that watery world, it was as though all the clocks had drowned too. But as the hot sun slowly worked its silent way across the sky, Purnama knew that morning had been a long time ago. He was getting very, very thirsty.

There was nothing to do but wait. The water still lapped all around them, although there were no more waves. The earth still trembled, but nothing like the quake that morning.

The water level was going down. Purnama could see that. Now the second-story windows were visible. There was no strong tide, but it was evident the water was flowing out toward the ocean again. That was a relief. In the long hours of waiting, Purnama had wondered if the land had sunk enough that now it would be below sea level, and what was once land would now be ocean. Nothing was rational or secure. Anything seemed possible.

He decided to leave when he could see below the sills of the first-floor windows. There was nothing he could do up here anymore. Somehow, the other two men had disappeared.

He jumped across to another roof. The house swayed beneath him, and he realized the quake and the flood had weakened it. He jumped back onto the tile roof and went to the other side. The adjoining house roof was lower, and he jumped down on it. It felt solid beneath him and he climbed down onto the next roof.

"Here is a rope to go down," a young man at the edge of the roof told him. Purnama used the rope and descended onto the wreckage below him.

A few people were slowly walking along the street in silence, their vacant faces mirroring the shock Purnama felt. Some of the survivors had most of their clothes ripped off, and dried blood showed where they had been injured. No one seemed to know what to do.

All around him lay wreckage from the earthquake and the flood. Black mud covered everything. The cars, the furniture, the roofs and all the debris were the same color—black.

The corpses were the same. Lying about in tortured shapes, they all were covered with the same black slime, blending in as just another part of the wreckage. The upturned faces of many showed too keenly the terror that had overtaken them. Grief and horror surged through Purnama at first as he worked his way among the dead, and then he became numb. There were just too many dead. Many of them were piled up against the walls of the houses. He could see where the wave had pushed them against the unyielding barriers and kept them there as more and more bodies had been washed on top of them. The piles of bodies, lying still and covered with mud, were too awful to take in. Purnama could not keep those images from being branded into his memory.

"Why am I alive? I should be there among the dead." The more destruction and devastation he saw, the greater his wonder that he was alive. There were so few survivors and so many casualties. Yes, it was truly a miracle that he was alive.

*   *   *

After being evacuated to Medan, Atika and her children stayed there for four months. They returned to Banda Aceh and now live in barracks beside the church house. Formerly used for Sunday school classes and a fellowship hall, the building is now filled with refugees, the women and children sharing rooms and the men in other rooms.

"This is where my house was," Atika told me, motioning to a level plot of land. The concrete floor was all that was left. "All the wreckage was taken away by huge machinery that cleared the land."

She stood silent for a moment. "This is where we will rebuild. I have applied with help organizations for assistance, and I was promised aid. But we do not know when. There are so many houses to build."

She looked down at her feet. "At first, after the flood, I did not want to live. While we stayed in Medan with my brother and his family, I became ill. The doctor said I had swallowed too much polluted water and it would take time to get it out of my system.

"I did not care. I knew by then that Senno had died, although we never found his body. At night I could not sleep because of the horrors that would come to me in my dreams. I would wake up, shaking from fright.

"Gradually I began to have spirit to live again. I knew God was not giving up on me and that I still had a purpose in this life. Today I can thank the Lord for allowing me to have my son and daughter with me. There are many who have no family. Many children have no parents, and many parents have only one or two children left. Others have lost husbands and wives. We all have suffered.

"But I choose to believe that, somehow, God knows what He is doing. I need Him more now than ever before. He is my only hope."

* * *

Somehow, the survivors from Purnama's congregation were able to assemble in the central part of the city, all with stories of loss and pain. However, because many of the people from their church lived all over the city and were from areas not destroyed by the flood, their losses were not as huge as they first thought.

"We lost eleven people," Purnama said, "five children and six adults. But many lost relatives and family members who were not part of our congregation. Cahya and his parents had taken refuge on the roof of the building and were saved.

"That evening after the flood, I suddenly felt weak and nauseated. I sat on the floor and began to shiver uncontrollably.

"'Lord, have I survived the flood only to die now from the dirty water I swallowed?' My mind was sluggish and I began to lose consciousness. My friends carried me to a house where I could rest.

I was sick all night, and people kept getting me to drink bottled water to try to flush my system.

"By the next day I was better, but still weak. Then I helped others looking for the bodies of the missing. We hunted five days, and then we had to evacuate to Medan because of the decomposing bodies and health hazards. It was getting impossible to find enough food and clean water for all the survivors. Banda Aceh was turning into a ghost town and people were breaking into stores and looting. It was chaotic."

Today, Purnama is back in Banda Aceh. "I have a work to do. Our congregation is growing as more and more people realize how insecure life is. It has brought a new awareness that we will not always be on this earth. All of us have looked into the face of death."

Now, as Purnama preaches, the people listen keenly. They know what it is to experience suffering. It is not difficult for the Acehnese to believe in the end times.

"When I was in Medan, someone on the street tried to get me to buy a CD of footage from the tsunami. I told him, 'I don't need a film of the tsunami. I was one of the people in the film. I don't need any more reminders of how it was during that time.'"

Two verses that Purnama clings to are Habakkuk 3:17-18: "Although the fig tree shall not blossom . . . and the fields shall yield no meat . . . yet I will rejoice in the Lord, I will joy in the God of my salvation."

3

Vantage Point

The garage was shady and cool compared to the street, where the early morning sun was already heating up the day. *Sinar* switched off the ignition and opened the door of the car. As he got out and walked around the front of his vehicle, he felt the floor shake.

"Earthquake!" he exclaimed. He stopped to get his balance, resting his right hand on the hood of the car.

Then, with a mighty heave, the floor tilted and the car slid toward him, threatening to pin him against the concrete wall. He whirled around and placed both hands on the front grill of the car, pushing it away from him. But the floor continued to tilt, until he had to push with all his might to keep from being crushed. "Help!" he called out, straining to protect himself.

Next door, he could hear his brother screaming and running out of the house.

"Help!" Sinar shouted again.

Parto came rushing in. "Leave your car and run out. Earthquake!"

"I'm pinned," Sinar tried to explain. For a brief moment, the floor dipped down again and Sinar pushed the rocking car away from him.

Then he was alone. He heard Parto yelling for his family to come out of the house. He must not have seen what was happening in the garage.

It was agony for the middle-aged man. The earth would shake, and Sinar was able to push the car away from his body enough to get some respite, but every time he tried to move away from the front, the car attacked him again like something alive. At times Sinar felt himself blacking out as he strained against the crushing deadweight.

All around him, he could hear people screaming. He heard the voice of his wife, *Vivi*, in their own house and tried to call out to her, but his strength was leaving him. "Help!" he called again, panic sweeping over him.

"Sinar!" It was his brother, Parto. "Where are you? Come out and leave the car. It is dangerous for you to be inside. Buildings are collapsing!"

Parto was staggering toward him. Just then the ground beneath them tilted the other way and the car rolled backward, away from the pinned man.

Sinar felt his strength ebb away. Everything began to whirl and a black cloud shut out the light. He slumped to the floor.

"Help, Sinar is hurt!" Parto yelled and dashed under the groaning roof to rescue his brother. He grabbed him under his arms and, straining, lifted the limp figure and dragged him away from the garage.

"What is it?" Vivi cried out. She tried to get up from her sitting position, but another quake sent her sprawling again. Parto slumped to the ground with his burden and said, "He has fainted!"

When Sinar became conscious, the ground beneath him was still rumbling and shaking. With a flash, his memory came back to him.

"Drink this," his wife said, holding a bottle of water to his mouth.

Sinar drank deeply, feeling the strength return to his body.

There was no time to explain what had happened. All around them, house walls were falling and roofs were collapsing. They could hear the screams of people over the creaking of strained timbers and the dull rumbling deep inside the earth. All was in chaos.

The screams coming from the house next door alarmed them. Why was their neighbor screaming so? Was she hurt? It sounded as though she was calling for help.

After the earth finally stopped heaving and shaking, the screaming continued. Their neighbor man came running up to them.

"Help!" he cried. "My little daughter is hurt."

They all ran around the side of their neighbor's house. Or what was left of the house. One corner had collapsed and the roof leaned toward the ground over the second floor. The cries were coming from inside.

Sinar gasped when he saw the gash on the little girl's leg. Blood was oozing out, in spite of the strip of cloth her mother had wrapped around it. The little girl was crying loudly.

"Can you take them to the doctor?" the neighbor man asked anxiously, plucking at Sinar's sleeve.

"My car is blocked by wreckage," Sinar replied. He tried to force his mind to think clearly.

"You could take the cycle," Vivi told her husband, looking at the woman. Then she said, "You are hurt too."

The lady did not say anything, but pleaded, "Please take my daughter to the doctor. The cut is very deep."

Pushing away debris, Sinar righted his cycle. With the woman holding her child in her arms behind him, he made his way to the doctor's house.

Parts of the city had hardly any damage, and in other parts the houses lay in ruins. Power poles leaned drunkenly against buildings, and wires sagged onto the ground.

They were not the only ones who had come to see the doctor. Others had brought their injured, and both the doctor and his wife were busy seeing to their needs. Sinar felt relieved when his neighbor and her daughter were safely in the doctor's care.

He turned his cycle to go back to his family. A dull ache throbbed at the base of his neck. He shook his head to clear his brain.

At the first cry of "Water!" from the rushing crowd on the street,

Tsunami!

Sinar knew what was happening. A tsunami! He was sure of it. An earthquake as massive as the one they had just experienced meant that a gigantic wave had been unleashed in the ocean and was coming into the city.

Sinar wanted to go back to his family to make sure they were going to be all right, but he knew he could not reach them in time. Tsunamis wait for no one.

He stopped his cycle beside the skeleton of a new three-story concrete building and dashed up the rough stairs. He heard the masses of people running on the streets and wanted to tell them to take refuge in some tall building, but there was no time and too much noise. He ran up the second flight of stairs, then the third, and, panting hard, came out onto the flat roof of the building. He looked toward the sea.

He looked past the fleeing crowds of people on the streets below him and on out toward the ocean. A wall of water towering more than two stories high was already sweeping over the land and heading in his direction.

From his vantage point, Sinar had a panoramic view of the catastrophe. He could clearly see boats and ships coming in on the crest of the wave, being tossed about like so many pieces of driftwood. He saw how the water hit the buildings, the waves splashing high over the roofs before pouring into the streets and alleys. The main wave came straight toward him. As the force of the wave pushed water up the parallel streets, Sinar watched as it dashed sideways down the alleys from both directions, trapping helpless people in the middle.

It all happened so devastatingly fast. Before he was aware of it, the water had risen up the walls of his building. The cars and tin roofs being swept along by the water made the wave look like liquid trash, hurtling along at breakneck speed and picking up anything in its path.

Sinar winced as he saw bodies flying through the air in the onslaught. The roaring, moaning, grinding monster was so noisy that only occasionally could he hear the screams of the victims. But he could see them.

Boats were tossed around in the angry waters. Some had keeled over, but others were still upright. A fishing vessel followed the wave, sailing along as though steered by the skipper.

A house was swept away by the wave and hurled toward the next building, the terrific impact demolishing both. This was happening all along the front of the wave, which swept away buildings as though they were made of matchsticks.

Then the wave hit his building. Sinar felt the building shudder under the impact, and waves dashed up toward him as the water divided around the tall building. Timbers creaked and groaned under the tremendous assault, and lumber splintered off and was added to the lethal wave. Like a gigantic blender, the waves swirled the debris madly about, cutting up anything weak and vulnerable.

The wave continued to push in toward the center of the city, slowing as it met resistance from all the debris and buildings.

Sinar did not know how far inland the water was reaching. He only knew he was no longer three stories above the water. All around him water covered many of the two-story buildings. Some rooftops were visible, with debris washed up on the tin and tile.

The earth continued to tremble beneath him, and Sinar sat down. Suddenly he felt old and tired. He numbly wondered what had happened to his family. Was it only a few minutes ago that he had taken his wounded neighbors to the doctor's house? It seemed more like hours ago.

Nothing like this had ever happened to him before. He couldn't think properly. What would happen next? Would it be days before he could be rescued? Would he ever be rescued? Was the city now going to be under water?

The hot sun beat down on him unmercifully. He looked dumbly at the water level as it fell slightly. Then he looked out toward the ocean again. What he saw made him tremble. Another wave was headed his way, the front of it rearing up like a sea monster, reaching out over the drowned city. Was this one going to be even higher?

The wave carried with it floating objects. Sinar saw a closed refrigerator tumble past, mostly submerged in the black, oily water.

And the boats! There were small fishing boats and larger sea vessels, all bobbing up and down on top of the water. Sinar saw that most of them were empty, swept loose from their moorings by the wave and now floating around at the whim of the currents.

Welcome clouds covered the sun and a brief shower brought some relief from the scorching heat. Sinar sat in a stupor, hardly daring to think what the next hours would bring. The sun came out again and beat down on the drowned city. Time dragged on.

While the afternoon hours crept by, Sinar saw the tide returning to the ocean. The boats began moving slowly toward the sea, but as the water level went down, many were beached on the streets or against houses, lying on their sides.

The receding water revealed far more than wreckage. Scattered throughout the surreal landscape were the bodies of men, women, and children, sprawled on the wreckage, half buried in the mud, or lying silently side-by-side. The area lay in ruins worse than any battle scene. The earthquake had begun the damage, but the tsunami had wreaked far greater havoc.

Easing his way back down to street level amid the wreckage took Sinar a long time. Again and again he was blocked by debris and had to find another way to exit the building.

When he got back down to the street, he walked back toward the city, still in a stupor. He met other survivors quietly weeping or walking around in a daze. Children, wide-eyed with fear, wandered aimlessly. Some sat down on the street, hopeless and with nowhere to go.

As he neared his own street, Sinar felt hope rise in his chest. Here the water had not been as high. He could see people moving around in second-story windows, and the farther he walked, the less damage he saw.

"Sinar!" He heard the glad cry of his wife's voice as he came up the street toward his house. Vivi was calling to him eagerly from the upstairs window of Parto's house. "Sinar is alive!" she turned to yell to the people inside the house.

Sinar is one of the few people I interviewed who had not lost any of his family. His house was closer to the center of the city and did not suffer as much damage from the flood as it did from the earthquake. His vantage point from the top of the three-story building close to the shore gave him a unique view as the tsunami swept over the city.

4

Bridging the Gap

I had no idea God was preparing me for this ministry when I was young. I know I used to resent the problems our family faced, living as Christians in Indonesia, where most of the population is Muslim.

You see, my father is a Christian pastor. I grew up poor. We had to move from place to place, because the Christian churches were very small and faced a lot of difficulties. I didn't mind the moving around; I knew nothing else. It was the poverty I minded.

I have one older sister and two younger ones. As young girls growing up, we all needed food, and many times there was very little to eat. Rice, that is what we ate most of all. My mother used to try to buy soybeans whenever she could to mix with the rice to give us some protein. To eat meat was an almost unheard of luxury in our family, unless we ate with a family far richer than we.

To understand the tensions in our country during my teenage years, you have to understand about the two main groups in Indonesia. There are the Muslims, which make up more than 80 percent of the population; the other 20 percent consists of Christians, Buddhists, and a few other religions. Even though there have been Christians in Indonesia for years, every so often an incident will spark an upheaval that throws the country into chaos.

When I was sixteen, trouble started brewing. It was December 1999. I was a schoolgirl, staying with my two younger sisters and my mother with our relatives. Father had gone to preach in several other churches, and my older sister, Audrey, was in the city of *Ternate*. My school sat close to the coastline in a Muslim area. We lived in the Christian area. I had to leave our area and enter the Muslim community to attend school with the other children from that town. This was nothing unusual; I had done that since elementary school.

That December, however, there were rumors that the Christians were going to have a "bloody Christmas." The Muslims actually started the rumor, and they openly talked about it when they were sure the Christians would hear them.

When I use the word *Christian*, I really refer to all the people who were called Christians simply because they were not Muslims. We are required to carry identity cards in Indonesia, and when police or government officials want to check our residency status, they ask to see our ID cards. On the card, beside our name and other vital statistics, is a space identifying our religion. Since the government officials are almost all Muslims, they want to know who is "loyal" to them and who is of another persuasion. People can register as Muslims, Buddhists, or Christians. If you are not a Muslim or a Buddhist, then you are given the religion of Christian. Even atheists are classed as Christian because they are not Muslims or Buddhists. So the word Christian becomes a derogatory term to the Muslims because of all the people classed as Christians, but not Christians at all. To them, "Christian" simply means "not a Muslim."

One day while I was in school, word reached us that in Ternate there had been a horrible massacre. Muslims had surrounded a church filled with people and had burned the church and the people inside. This news spread throughout all the islands of Indonesia, and tensions mounted.

In spite of the tension, I continued to go to school. Mother and my two sisters moved to another house, but because it was farther from school, I stayed where I was. We all worried about Audrey, who was in the middle of the trouble.

On January 4, my aunt awakened me at four o'clock in the morning. "The Muslims are attacking us! Hurry!"

Terrified, I jumped out of bed and got dressed. "Vehicles are taking us to a safe place," my aunt told me quickly.

Because our area was right next to a heavily populated Muslim area, we were in danger. Even while leaving, we could see lights and hear men shouting in the distance. Bright flashes of fire indicated where they were burning houses.

I had never been so scared in my life. I fully expected our vehicle to be stopped by armed Muslims as we raced through the night.

We drove about three miles to another section of the city farther from the seacoast. There we joined others who had fled, and the vehicles left to get those still in danger.

All that day, rumors flew around like cannon balls. We were told that the Christian men had taken guns and were defending our part of the city. Then we heard that the Muslims had burned so many Christian houses that an entire block was on fire. Word reached us that the Muslims had gone crazy with madness and had gone to the Christian cemetery and were destroying the burial ground.

There was a lot of praying going on in the house where I stayed. I prayed, too—mostly for the safety of my family. I did not know how my mother and younger sisters were faring and my vivid imagination had them all killed. Where was my father? How was Audrey in Ternate, where the trouble had begun?

Of course I knew about prayer. My parents had prayed for as long as I could remember. So when this terrible threat came into my life, I prayed, though I was not sure if God heard me or not. I comforted myself with the thought that somehow God must be on our side, for surely, as Christians, we had a closer relationship with God through Jesus. Were we not being persecuted for being Christians?

That evening, there was a huge commotion out in the street. We women and children all flocked outside to see what was happening. There I saw something I will never forget.

A vehicle full of men with guns was slowly coming up the street.

The men were cheering wildly, waving their guns in the air. As the crowds lining the streets saw what the vehicle was dragging, they began to cheer and wave their arms madly. "Victory, victory, victory!"

Then the vehicle came closer. I saw something being dragged by a rope tied to the rear bumper. It was a dead man!

Word flew from mouth to mouth. It was the captain of the Muslims who had attacked the Christians! The Christians had defeated the murdering Muslims and driven them back to the seacoast. The people were delirious with joy.

I am sure some of the more sane ones knew this was but a small victory. We all knew we were outnumbered. With what kind of new violence would the Muslims now punish us for killing their leader?

As everyone milled around and stories flew about how we had shown the Muslims that we were not going to be pushed around by them, I kept wondering where my mother and sisters were.

We stayed there for over a week with no further incidents. Neither side dared create more trouble. Someone told my aunt that her house had not been destroyed, and we actually moved back.

We still had not heard anything from my family. I often wondered if I was now an orphan, for there was no way to communicate with each other. I did not dare ask anyone about it for fear of finding out that they had all been killed. It was better not knowing and still hoping they would someday appear than knowing they were dead.

One day a car stopped in front of my aunt's house, and I heard a babble of voices. I heard my mother call out for me. I dashed outside and there were my father, my mother, and my two younger sisters! I ran into their arms and wept for joy. Something inside my chest crumpled, and I could not stop crying. I thought I would collapse.

"There, there," Father comforted us women. "God has truly protected us all. At least He has brought most of us through without harm." I knew then that they did not know if Audrey was safe or not.

"Tomorrow we must leave," Father told us. "This is not a safe place for us. We will go to *Manado*."

Manado was a city that was mostly Christian. It was considered the safest place in all of Indonesia for Christians. The Muslims wanted all the Christians to leave their areas and settle together, away from them.

I felt relieved. Surely in Manado we could be safe. But could we get there safely? What dangers would we face as we passed through Muslim-controlled areas to get to our destination? I knew that, as a well-known pastor, my father was a wanted man.

"We have to try to find Audrey first," my father decided. "I know of a place in the forest where you can stay while I go to Ternate for Audrey."

"Father, I will go with you," I spoke up passionately. "Let me go with you, please!"

Father hesitated. He looked a long time at me and then decided. "All right. First, we will all go to the lumber camp where many other refugees are staying. There are armed guards protecting that camp all the time. Then you and I will go to find Audrey."

We went by ship. I could not enjoy a single part of the trip to Ternate, because there were all kinds of other ships on the sea and we never knew if they were filled with Muslims or not. We continued to hear of terrible clashes between the two sides, and even the ship we were on had cannons to try to protect us. We flew the red flag to indicate we were Christians.

When we entered the harbor at Ternate, we were told that whatever business we had to do had to be done in less than thirty minutes, for it was not safe to stay there very long.

My father and I ran up the street to where Audrey had been boarding. How grateful we were to find her at home! She grabbed her belongings and we raced back to the boat.

There were no major incidents on the way back. As soon as we arrived back in the lumber camp, we took another boat to Manado. That journey took us three days and I got sick. I remember vomiting and feeling as though all my insides were coming up. I think part of my illness was due to my nerves. I was very thankful to finally reach Manado.

Would I have been so glad had I known what awaited us there?

At first, it was not too bad. We stayed with some church people for two days and were able to rest and recount our experiences as a family. There was food to eat. I could have stayed there longer except more and more people kept coming. Father decided we had to leave to make room for the waves of refugees that kept coming.

So we went to the refugee camp. Here were thousands of refugees living in orderly ranks of tents. For our meals we stood in line with bowls to get the instant noodles and rice that were our main food.

The chief enemy in refugee camps is boredom. There is nothing to do. There are so many people that it is impossible to organize anything. Everyone is crowded together, and there is no one to really care about what is happening to you. Finally you feel you are just one little ant in a swarming anthill.

We lived there for more than two years. We had food to eat and a place to sleep. My father became active in the evangelistic services that different churches planned for us. He was gone a lot, and my mother was left to try to keep us girls in order.

Teenagers roamed the camps and I joined them. Audrey did not seem as restless as I was, and my younger sisters found their own friends.

How did beer ever get into the camp? I don't know, but there was a lot of partying and I joined right in. I felt as though I was caught in a quicksand of monotony and wanted something new and exciting to do.

My parents were grieved with my activities and tried to talk to me. I ignored them and spent as little time in our tent as possible. I did not understand their world, and I was sure they did not understand mine.

One common thread that bound our group was our hatred of the Muslims. We knew they were to blame for all our troubles. We spent hours and days planning revenge and wishing all kinds of ills on the entire tribe. We felt sure that God was on our side. Even those who did not profess any kind of religion were sure that somehow we were the favored ones. We felt quite zealous and discussed many political ideologies among ourselves.

"There is a group of people coming in to have meetings at the center," someone informed us one day. "They call themselves 'Abba Love.' "

"They must be on our side then," someone decided. "Abba means Father God and God is for us, so that is good."

"I want to see what it is all about," I decided. "Let's go!"

It was the beginning of interesting meetings, even though the young people who sang and spoke to us did not get into politics. There was something about them that was different. Their approach to life was unlike anything I had ever known.

For one thing, they were Indonesians like us, so they could identify with our culture, and we could hear from their testimonies that they were not spoiled rich children who had led privileged lives. Many were from *Jakarta*, but there were some from other areas.

When they spoke about Jesus, it was not how He was displeased with people. It was more what they themselves had experienced with Christ. They talked about their struggles and how they overcame problems. If there were things they were still trying to overcome, they told us. I did not get the impression that these people were perfect, but rather that they were on a journey toward perfection.

I felt something inside my heart respond to the kind of experience they talked about. I wished I had some way of knowing how to deal with the problems I faced. However, I was not sure what my friends would think. Many of us attended the meetings, but we didn't talk about them much. We just attended.

Then they began telling us about a discipleship program they were offering. In this program, there would be extra meetings for those who were truly interested in knowing God in a deeper way. They announced that classes would begin the next week.

I did not tell anyone, but I went. Even now I am not sure just what my reason was for joining. I was bored, and any kind of meeting was better than doing nothing, but that wasn't all. Perhaps I wanted to see if I could make new friends. Whatever the reason, I began going regularly.

They began talking about deeper issues—anger, hatred, bitterness, and rebellion. In clear and simple teaching, they exposed what happens when people allow their hearts to become enslaved with these vices.

I knew they spoke the truth. It was extremely clear, for all around us were living—and dead—examples. The bloodshed, the carnage, the retaliation between warring factions—all of these proved their point.

It was when they began talking about the remedy that I became uneasy. I did not understand. I told myself I was a Christian. Wasn't that why we had been driven from our homes by the Muslims and massed together in this camp? Weren't we suffering for Christ?

In March, we were invited to a retreat. This would last for four days, and we would spend all day and every evening in teaching sessions.

I went. It was held just outside the camp. The teaching was intense and the speakers did not spare anyone. We were all made to look deep inside our hearts and see who we really were.

They also spoke very plainly to us and told us being Christians was not enough. They rightly said that there are thousands of "Christians" who are as wicked and unhappy as anyone else and yet feel as though somehow God is blessing them. They explained that, unless we repent from our own sins and find that Jesus is the answer to our needs, being "Christian" is not enough.

These thoughts were new to me. I began seeing how many of us in the camp were very wrong in our thinking. We thought our belief that Jesus is the Son of God made us all right. But I saw I had never made Jesus the Lord of my life. I had said I believed in Him, but really I only said I believed He existed. Now I heard that I needed to receive His nature into my heart. I was to be like Him!

I had come to the point that I wanted to be a real Christian. There was no longer any doubt that the only way to God was through Jesus, but I battled with my bitter thoughts against the Muslims who had fought against our people, and I still hated them for what they had done.

"Tell God exactly what you feel. He knows it already, but it will do you good to hear yourself say what you feel. This is being honest with yourself. Then ask Him to help you forgive." The young man spoke sincerely to our class.

The last day of the retreat, the message was on the sacrifice Jesus had made for us. I no longer thought of the life of Jesus as something that had only happened in the past; I was now thinking of Him as with us in the present. It made a difference. Jesus was becoming a real person for me.

When I heard again how Jesus was abused, misunderstood, rejected by His own people, and finally crucified, something broke inside of me. I began to weep.

A group of us stayed after the meeting. We were all weeping and praying. For the first time, I let go of my feelings completely and asked Jesus to cleanse me from all my doubts, my hatred, and my feelings of superiority. I wanted nothing more than to allow Christ to come into my life and make me a new person.

After the retreat, I went back into camp. I went home and told my family what had happened. With joy, my parents accepted my apologies and together we worshipped.

Now I had a purpose in life. I had a reason to exist! I wanted to do anything I could for my Lord, my Saviour.

I became active in the Abba Love group and spoke to other youth about my experiences. I joined an accountability group in which three of us girls met regularly to pray and to open our lives to each other for examination.

Less than a year later, we left the camp. We were able to relocate and my father continued his work as a pastor. I continued my schooling.

At first, it was awkward for the Muslim and Christian youth to attend the same schools, and we basically avoided each other. But the Spirit spoke to me, and I began to seek ways of becoming friends with the Muslim girls. I tried to avoid doing things that antagonized them and sought out ways I could help them with their studies. I actually became friends with several of them.

Then the opportunity came for me to go to Jakarta and take an intensive six-month training course with the Abba Love group. Those months were a great help in my Christian life. During that time I was able to go back to the village where I had lived with my aunt and help people, Muslims as well as Christians, rebuild their houses. We held meetings for the young people and shared our testimonies.

Then, in December 2004, the tsunami hit our country.

Although I was not directly affected by the tsunami, everyone in Indonesia was somehow moved by the catastrophe. At church, we prayed fervently and asked God how we could respond in a way that would turn people to Him.

Barely five months later a group was sent to Banda Aceh to help in the rebuilding process. I was asked to accompany them.

Now, as I am here helping the Acehnese rebuild their city, I see how God was preparing me all through my youth for this experience. I have never seen destruction on the scale that happened here in Aceh. The first time I saw all the houses leveled by the waves, I could not speak. I just stared. I had seen houses burned by the fighters, but that was nothing to this. All the pictures I had seen, all the stories I had read—nothing had prepared me for the startling reality I now saw.

Now we are helping the Acehnese rebuild. We are showing the love of Jesus to the people, not in preaching and teaching, but by coming and helping them in the practical areas of life.

At first when the Muslims find out we are Christians, they are not sure how they should respond. Many have never really known Christians for this is a predominantly Muslim city.

As time goes on, they see we are people just as they are. We learn to grieve with them and laugh with them. They learn to trust us and hopefully find out that many of their ideas about Christians were wrong.

We have our times of fellowship and devotions among the twenty or so people who live together. We invite our new friends to eat with us and to go places with us. We ask them about the best places to get building materials, and we employ them as drivers and workers for the projects.

When is the time to present the Gospel to them? When should we begin the evangelization work?

That is the timing of the Spirit. We know that now we are to build relationships by helping them. We are not here to condemn, to make them feel we are superior, but to show the love of Jesus by living it. We pray that God will open the hearts of the Acehnese and speak to them through Jesus, the only true way to God.

For me, I am happy to be in the work of the church. I love Jesus in a way I never knew possible, and I am strengthened daily by the close fellowship I have with the other believers here. I do not know how long we will be here or what we will do next. I just know I am perfectly satisfied to be in this work, and I trust my future to the Lord.

5

An Old Woman

It's over. I mean, the tsunami. I have a tendency to call the tsunami "it." I guess it's because it made such a huge impact on my life, and on my family's life. The family that is left over. The few of us who survived.

Though I was an old woman before it hit, I am even older now. I know that might sound funny, because of course everyone gets older every year, but really, I am much older now. I feel as though this catastrophe has aged me more than ten years. I feel at least a hundred years old.

Before it came, we were a large family. There were my husband and I, our four children and their spouses, and our nine grandchildren. Life in Banda Aceh was never easy for us, but we had our jobs, our houses, and plenty to eat.

When I first felt the earth shake on that Sunday morning, I thought it would soon end. Earthquakes are not exactly common, but I had experienced several in my lifetime. The earth usually shook a little, and then it was over. At times there had been some damage, but nothing major. Not, however, that we ever got used to the earth shaking beneath our feet.

I knew we were in for a major quake when I was thrown down

as I was crossing the kitchen floor. I banged against the side of the table and hurt my arm. As I sat on the floor, I heard my husband, *Dono*, calling for me.

"Come out, *Ridha*. Earthquake!"

I already knew that, of course, but when something happens very suddenly, you do not think about what you are saying.

I pulled myself up, grasping the edge of a chair, and steadied myself against the wall. I went into the main room of our house. Things were flying off the shelves onto the floor and the entire house was shaking and groaning. Added to this was a deep, underground rumbling, as though some giant was extremely angry.

The quake did not slow down; in fact, it increased. Holding onto my husband's arms, I staggered out the door and went to the middle of the street where others from our neighborhood were gathered.

There were not very many people crying out, though I could hear muted cries of alarm as the earth continued to shake everything back and forth. I think we were too scared to say anything. There is not much you can say when the whole world is tossing and turning below you.

"Sit down," Dono instructed me, and we sat right down on the heaving blacktop.

Then the real trouble started. We had been afraid of the earthquake, but only because we did not know that something much worse was coming.

The wave was still more than fifteen feet high by the time it reached our part of town. Dono and I, along with most of our family, were still outside. We heard people yelling, "Water! Water is coming!" and it confused us terribly. Then we saw the wall of water come rushing toward us, and suddenly, we were in it.

I vaguely remember being tossed upward as though I was as light as a doll, and then I was under water, tossed and turned by the rushing wave. Not only water, but broken pieces of wood and cars and furniture and cycles and anything imaginable. Debris hit my body, and as I was swept along, I felt myself being pushed against something hard.

It was a water pipe running up the outside of a house. I grabbed hold with all my might as the water continued to swirl around me. I sputtered and gasped as I tried to keep my head above water. I cannot swim, and I really thought I would drown.

As I struggled to keep my grip on the water pipe, my first thoughts were about our family. Where was Dono? Where were the children and grandchildren?

I could hardly think. I was so confused, and there was black water all around me, drowning the city. Nothing seemed real. I was living a nightmare.

I do not know how long I clung to that water pipe, but my feet found something fairly solid beneath me and I just stayed there, praying with all my might.

The time becomes blurred after that. I do not remember how I found my husband, but sometime after the water level finally went down, I was with Dono.

Our clothes were wet and filthy from the water, and an oily film was all through my hair.

"Your leg is cut!" I told Dono as I saw red blood oozing out and trailing across his dirty leg.

"Where?" he asked dully, looking down at where I was pointing.

There was nothing to clean his cut with, nothing to use to bandage it. I began examining myself, and miraculously, I did not have any serious cuts, although I knew I would bruise in several places where something heavy had hit me.

"Thank God we survived," I murmured. Yet I was worried. Where were the rest?

It turned out that there were not many of us left. Besides Dono and I, one of our daughters-in-law and two of our grandchildren survived. There were now only five of us.

For the next several days we searched among the dead and wounded, hoping to find some family member. We only found three-year-old Mona. That is, we found her body.

For some reason, finding one member made us all the more determined to look for the rest. We hunted and hunted, searching among the hundreds of corpses, but finally we gave up. We buried little Mona up close to the mountains where the water had not reached. There was no one to help except our family. Everyone else was too busy, either burying their dead, or hunting for lost family members.

By the third day, the smell was becoming unbearable. So right after we had buried Mona, we left for Medan by airplane.

Dono's leg had begun to swell. As soon as we were in Medan, he was taken to a hospital, along with hundreds of other wounded people. The staff was overworked. Day after day, they tried to take care of the wounded and ill. I sat beside my husband's cot and watched as he became weaker and weaker.

One morning I noticed he was trying to say something, but he was too weak. I laid my hand on his forehead, and his skin was dry and hot to my touch. When I finally found a nurse, she came with me and took his temperature. I noticed how tired she looked, and yet she was trying to help me.

Two hours later, Dono was transported to another hospital where a different doctor examined him.

"His entire system is poisoned," he told me after the examination. "He has taken in toxins from the polluted water. He must have swallowed a lot to get in this condition."

I watched his condition worsen day by day. He became delirious. A week after we arrived in Medan, he died. I guess I was in a state of shock, because I really did not react much when I realized he was dead.

Someone helped me arrange for his burial. My daughter-in-law and a few from her family who had survived came with the two grandchildren. The funeral was brief and small. The pastor from a church in Medan conducted the graveside service, and although we did not know him, we felt privileged to have him there.

Christian workers were very busy. They were trying to help us displaced people by providing places for us to stay and helping us with food and clothes. But there were so many of us. So many, and yet so few.

I stayed in Medan for four months. Then I heard that the survivors from my church had returned, and I decided to return to Banda Aceh. Someone had told me that none of our houses had survived, so when I came back, I immediately went to our church house.

Thankfully, the building had survived. The fellowship hall had been converted to a housing unit, and this is where I now live.

I do not know what will happen now. My daughter-in-law lives with her relatives and I occasionally see her and the two grandchildren. But most of the time I am alone. Alone and old. So old.

My mind often goes back over my life. I realize I had a good life before the tsunami and I am grateful for what I had. That is where I mostly live—in the past. I dwell in the times when I had a life and a family and things were normal. To live in the present is very painful—too painful to even feel. I seldom cry, but sometimes when I wake at night I know I have been crying in my sleep. My bed sheets are wet and I feel as though I have been swimming in water all night long.

I still have my few friends. We talk about the past and try to see what we can do to help those who survived. Sometimes we take care of the children while the adults try to rebuild their houses or find work or get food. There are humanitarian workers who assist us with food. God is very gracious to allow us to receive this help. Without it, I don't know how anyone could survive.

Survive. It is strange to use that word, because it seems to be such an uncertain one. After the tsunami, I was comforted by the fact that at least Dono and I had both survived, but now he is gone. I wonder how long I will survive? Many days it doesn't matter. I just live from day to day, taking whatever comes, trying to exist.

My greatest and only comfort is my faith. I do believe in God, though I have no idea why He allowed all this to happen. The faith I have in the Lord is all that is left to me. I have felt the presence and comfort of God. I know many do not have that, and it must be terrible. Others in our church have comforted me.

So, I have hope. Hope in Jesus Christ. One day, when we see Him face to face, we will have perfect rest. I have confidence my family that perished is with God in heaven and I long to see them all.

This is my story. The story of an old woman.

6

I Change Gods

As soon as I entered my house, I heard *Eti* singing.

> Jesus, you are the strength of my life,
> I trust in you, I believe in you,
> You hold me in your loving arms.
> Jesus, my joy, my song!

Singing at a time like this! I knew quite well that my daughter was as scared as I was of earthquakes. Now she was singing. How was it possible?

I paused before our household shrine and bowed my head reverently toward the little holy statue. I prayed a quick prayer for all of us. Even as I prayed, my eyes surveyed the barbershop I had on the first floor of our house. No major damage, I decided, then I went up the stairs.

"Grandma!" *Fifa* cried, running toward me. I wrapped my arms around my two-year-old grandson, Eti's son.

"Who is it?" Eti asked as she opened the bathroom door slightly and peered out. "Oh, Mama, it is you! Is Great-grandmother all right?"

"Yes, she is fine. Her house is slightly damaged, but nothing major." I sat down and drew Fifa to my side. "Aren't you worried?" I asked my daughter. "There have been more earthquakes."

"Oh, Mama," Eti lifted her big, dark eyes to me. "You know how I feel about earthquakes. Yes, I am scared!"

"Then why were you singing? I heard you singing as soon as I came home from my mother's."

"I have to sing," Eti said passionately. "There is nothing that encourages me more when I am scared than to sing some song to Jesus. He has promised to be with me all the time."

I shook my head and said nothing. It would do no good. Three years ago she had come home from Jakarta, and her life had been different ever since. A group of university students had held meetings and told the other students about this Jesus. She told us she became a believer in Jesus. *Okky*, her husband, started going to church with her several months later, and they often talked to us about what they believed. It didn't make sense to me. I had never heard of a god like Jesus. All our ancestors were Buddhists, and I did not dare leave our worship of the gods and our ancestors.

"They can't hear you," Eti would tell me when I lit candles before the statues and prayed my daily prayers. "Pray to a living God."

One day I got mad at her and told her to stop her chattering. I would do as I pleased and she could do as she pleased. After that, she did not say much.

"The bedroom window is broken," my youngest daughter, *Venna*, announced as she came out of the room she shared with Eti and Fifa. "There is glass all over the place."

I got up to see. Fifa tried to run ahead of us.

"No, Fifa," Eti called out. "Don't go in there. You will get cut."

Fifa stopped and looked at me. "No," I agreed. "Stay here."

Another quake sent us reeling toward the walls. "Should we go outside?" Venna asked anxiously. "Like we did the other time?"

The earth quieted. I shook my head. "I don't think it will be as strong as the other one. I hope not. I saw lots of damage on the way back from Great-grandma's house."

My mind went back to my aged mother who lived a city block away. After the severe quake that morning, I had hurried over to make sure she was not hurt.

"I will go and light the candles in front of the household gods," I told my daughters. "Clean up the broken glass and be careful not to get cut."

I was deeply moved by the earthquakes and there was unrest in my heart. I just did not know what was going to happen now. I would pray that our gods would protect us from any major damage.

Downstairs, *Fitri* was cleaning up the mess from the earthquake. She had worked for us for more than five years and was a part of our household. Since Okky was working in an inland city where he had gotten a job, Eti and Fifa also lived with us.

I began murmuring a prayer for protection as I lit a match and held it to the wick of a candle. Then, I went to the next one.

A noise outside arrested my attention. What was all the screaming about?

Standing in the open door, I looked outside. At first I saw nothing unusual except a whole flock of birds flying just above the street, heading away from the sea. But the shouts came closer.

I stepped out into the street so I could see better.

A crowd of screaming people was being chased by a huge moving mass, like a bank of liquid earth two stories high. It was a flood!

I dashed inside, screaming at Fitri to follow me, and we ran upstairs.

"Run up to the fourth floor!" I screamed to my daughters. "Quick! A flood is coming!"

Eti grabbed Fifa and looked wild-eyed at me. "A flood?"

"There is no time. We must run!"

We panicked as we heard a horrible grinding noise coming closer and the terrified screams of people. Up the steps to the third floor we ran. This level was used mostly for storage, but we did not stay there. We went on up to the fourth floor, which was hardly more than an attic.

We were only up there for a minute before the flood hit our

house.

I will not forget the next several moments. The screams and cries of the people outside were terrible to hear. And the rush of water carrying along cars and roofs and junk made such an incredible noise I cannot describe it.

Our house is one of a whole row of houses built against each other in our city, and I guess that is what saved us. The water came with a mighty roar down the street in front of us and also in the alley behind us.

We huddled in the middle of the attic, all five of us. The noise outside kept on and on. Then, there was another earthquake—a series of shakes and quakes that made my insides turn into liquid. I had never been so afraid in my entire life.

Fitri was wailing. I heard another voice screaming, and suddenly realized it was my own. Venna had her head in my lap and was shaking in terror.

I looked at Eti. There she was with her eyes closed, her lips moving silently. I knew she was praying to her God.

I began screaming out to our gods to save us. I was so frantic, I wanted to do anything that would help us. I felt I would fly apart.

My mother! Great-grandma! Whatever was happening to her?

"Jesus, we are in your hands," Eti prayed. "Please be with us during this terrible time. Forgive our sins. Jesus, I place my life into your hands. Death is all around us and I don't know if this is the end of the world or not, but Jesus, I trust in you!" I could hear the words of Eti's prayer as she pressed Fifa to her breast.

The house trembled, not from the earthquake anymore, but from being hit by heavy objects outside. The noise of the rushing water was not down on the street; it was just outside the attic openings! Below us, I could hear glass breaking and water gushing inside. How high would the water rise? Was it already in the third floor? Would it continue to rise?

Most of all, I wondered about my mother. I could not imagine how she could survive a horrible flood like this. Her house was only two stories high. How could an eighty-year-old woman cope with a disaster like this? I screamed as I thought of her all by herself.

We huddled together, crying in fear. I repeated over and over again, "God of the earth and sea, save us! Save us!" I did not know what else to do.

Perhaps thirty minutes later I finally crept over to the window to look outside. What a horrible scene met our eyes as we peered down to where our street used to be. Dirty, oily water with junk floating on the surface was higher than the two-story windows. Some of the houses had only their roofs showing. I screamed in fear.

Venna took one look and jerked back. "Oh, Mama! Where are all the people?"

"Come away," I ordered everyone. "It is too terrible to see." I pulled on Eti's sleeve and motioned with my head toward little Fifa. "He should not see how it looks."

Fifa's eyes were all red from crying, and he rubbed his little chubby fists against his face. "Mama!" he wailed.

Eti drew him to her chest and felt his forehead. She looked at me. "He is hot."

"We are all hot up here in the attic," I told her, brushing sweat away from my forehead. The tin roof right above our heads was radiating the heat with intensity.

"What has happened?" Fitri quavered. "Are the gods of the sea angry?"

"It must be a tsunami," Eti told us. "I read in the university about such occurrences after earthquakes. Japan has had many tsunamis."

"Will the water go down?" Venna asked. "Will the sea stay in the city?"

No one had answers. I could not understand how it was possible for the sea to rise this much in the first place. It was over two stories high here. How high had it been along the seacoast?

Fitri crept over to the window again. She was soon back, hiding her face in her hands. "I saw a dead body floating on the water. It is terrible out there."

With every shake of the earth beneath us, we tried to prepare for some new catastrophe. We could hear the water occasionally rush through the street outside.

It was strange not to hear any traffic or any voices. It made the situation even more eerie. The only sounds were the rumbles of the earth beneath us and the slosh of water and heavy objects bumping against the side of our building.

I wondered if we were the only people left alive. How could we ever survive?

"I'm hungry," Fifa wailed.

"Fitri, go see if the third floor is flooded," I told our worker. "I had some instant noodles stored there."

Fitri drew in her breath sharply and I realized she was too frightened. I got up from the floor, opened the door that led to the stairs, and went down. Partway down, I stopped and gasped in despair.

Something had smashed a window and the black, oily water had washed inside, flooding the storage area to a depth of two feet. Everything on the bottom two shelves was completely ruined. I stood there in dumb amazement. Venna came down the stairs behind me and screamed in alarm. "Oh, this is horrible!"

An old sofa was sitting in the dirty water, the upholstery soaked. Suitcases half floated on the floor, pushed up against the wall.

Along to my right, we had built shelves, and on those shelves I had put my extra food supplies. The noodles were there, safely stored on the fourth shelf.

Then, with a grateful heart, I saw that my portable gas cooking plate was there too, unharmed by the flood. Perhaps we could use it later.

I took two plastic bags of instant noodles and carried them upstairs. "Look what I found."

Eti opened a package and Fifa hesitantly munched on the crisp noodles. Then, with a sniffle, he ate some more.

All day long we sat in our attic. Occasionally someone would creep over to the window and look out.

"It looks as though the water is going down," Eti said softly. Fifa had fallen asleep, and she had placed him on the floor on top of her jacket.

I marveled at my oldest daughter. She seemed the most calm and peaceful of us all.

All her growing-up years, Eti had been the timid one. She never did anything by herself, but was always hovering around others and letting her friends try out new things. She was most comfortable just watching. It was not that she was bashful. She had many friends and was very chatty and talked a lot. It was only that she was easily frightened—by thunderstorms, spiders, mad dogs. Anything.

Now, when something truly frightening had happened, she was the calmest of us all. I knew she was scared, for her eyes were large, and her face showed the strain she was under. But there was something else—something I did not understand. It was as though she had a peace in spite of the terrible things that were happening.

I certainly didn't. I had never been so scared in my life. I was sure we were all going to die in that attic. I fully expected another huge wave would come and drown us all or that our house was going to shake apart in one of the quakes that kept on scaring us all day. I felt sure our life on earth was over.

Many times I wondered what would happen after death. To me, death has always been a black, scary hole that nobody understood. I believed that the dead were all around us—unhappy, wandering souls that haunted the night and lived in the mountains. That is why I kept on adding more and more household gods. Whenever I found a new one, I would buy it and make a place for it somewhere. I must have had ten Buddhas, most of them small ones.

Now I wondered what had happened to all those gods. Were they drowned? How could I pray to them if they were under water? I desperately wanted something stable, something real. I felt as though I had nothing. I was the oldest, the mother. I should have been able to help my family. But I had nothing.

Fifa woke up and cried for water. This really scared me. We were all thirsty, sitting in the hot attic. I licked my dry lips.

Water. Why had I not brought some water up here before we came up? Such a foolish thought. There had been no time to think of such things. We just had to escape the drowning flood.

"The food shop," Eti said softly. "They sell bottled water." She looked at me.

I went to the window. Shadows were now filling the flooded

street, but I could see that the water had gone way down. The first-floor windows were now visible.

The food shop had junk piled up against the one end, but it looked as though there was a clearing just outside the front door.

The landscape looked surreal from our attic. Everything—all the overturned cars, the trash, the debris that littered the street—was covered with a black, oily film that obliterated all color and made objects appear shapeless.

"He feels feverish," Eti said later as she held her listless son. "We must get water." Then she closed her eyes and I knew she was praying.

"I will go and see if I can get some water," she said several minutes later. She got to her feet and handed Fifa to me.

"Eti," I said to her, "Is it . . . is it safe?"

"Mama," she said, her voice calm, determined, "I have to get something for Fifa. I have prayed and I know Jesus will be with me."

Once again I marveled at my daughter. At one time she would not go to the market by herself for fear a stray dog would attack her. Now she was willing to wade through the mud, debris, broken glass, and dead bodies we had seen to get water for her son. I realized Eti had a strength I did not know she possessed. I saw her close her eyes once more and pause for a few moments. Then she left.

We waited in silence. Fifa whimpered in my arms, and Venna kept glancing at her wristwatch. Fitri toyed with the buttons on her blouse.

"I saw the gas cooking plate in the storage room," I remembered out loud. "If Eti can find water, we can cook our noodles instead of eating them right out of the package."

It seemed like a long time before we heard someone come upstairs. It was Eti, clutching an armful of water bottles. With a white face, she cleaned one of the bottles and opened it. Gratefully little Fifa drank deeply, then we all had a drink.

Eti's breast rose and fell as though she had been running. I looked at her curiously. She seemed unable to speak.

I decided to find something downstairs to cook the noodles in.

Now that we had water, our future did not seem as bleak. I rummaged around and found a cooking pot and several empty containers we could use as plates. We drank the noodles, for there were no spoons.

The comforting smell of cooking noodles made our nightmare seem more bearable. Fifa fell asleep as darkness crept into the attic, and we sat in the silence. Earlier we had heard some voices outside, but now there was no noise. Just an eerie quietness as though we were in some ghost town.

"It was terrible," Eti said in a low voice. "There are drowned people everywhere on the street. Inside the shop, there is so much mud that I had to search and search before I found the water."

"Was there plenty there?" I asked eagerly.

"Yes. No one else has been there to get any. There was probably some other stuff there, too, but I did not know if it was right to get it. I even felt guilty taking the water without paying for it. I will pay the clerk, if . . . when . . ." Eti's voice trailed away into silence.

That night was miserable, trying to sleep on the hard, wooden boards and being wakened by wild dreams. The awful trauma of what we had gone through took its toll on all of us.

The next morning, before light stole into our attic window, I was awake. I lay there wondering what we were going to do. Would there be another flood? Earthquakes still shook the house occasionally, but with less intensity.

I realized Eti was awake too. I could hear her whispering and I strained to hear.

"Lord, I do not know why you have allowed this terrible thing to happen to us. I pray for Fifa. You know he is sick. I pray for our family. I pray for Great-grandmother. My mind is numb and I do not know what to pray for. I pray for your mercy on us here in this attic. Please, God, take away the fear that wants to make me panic. Take away the images of the dead I saw yesterday." Her voice went on and on.

I knew she was praying to her God. I knew it, and somehow, I wished my gods would be so . . . so friendly like that. How would it be to be able to talk to someone like that about my personal fears and wants? I feared my gods and never felt they were really interested in my life. I only knew I must try to make them happy with me by lighting the candles and placing the offerings of food before them.

They never ate the food. They never indicated that anything I did ever pleased them. Whenever we had good luck, I felt somehow I had pleased them. But I never believed that they took a personal interest in me. Sometimes I felt they could favor me and other times they weren't interested.

But Eti's God was her friend! I could tell by how she talked to Him.

Somehow we made it through that day and through the night. Then another day. And another night.

The second time Eti went to get water, she could not eat or drink for a long time afterwards. We did not need to ask why. The horrible stench of rotting flesh reached into the attic.

The third day, we were surprised by voices in our house below us. I went to investigate, calling out, "Who is there?"

We heard scrambling as the intruders left and I realized someone had been checking our house for something worth stealing. It made me mad. We had suffered enough from the flood without having looters take what little might be salvageable.

On the fourth day, I made a decision. We would try to leave. We could not survive forever in this hideaway. For one thing, we were running low on food. Eti brought some things back from the store, and we had more than just the instant noodles, but we knew the stench would make it unbearable for us to stay.

"We have to leave," I said to Eti, holding my hand over my mouth. "We will all get sick from the disease that will spread from the dead."

She nodded and we went down from the attic.

The journey out was worse than anything I had ever experienced. I tried not to look at the dead, but it was impossible not to see them. The corpses were everywhere. It was like something would just grab my eyes and make me look at them—bodies half buried in the stinking mud, bloated to twice their normal size. Babies lying in their mothers' arms. I could barely see at first as tears blinded my eyes.

We were all crying. At first I had wanted to go see if my mother was somehow all right, but after a few minutes of picking our way through the debris, all I wanted was to get out of there.

We walked about two miles, and then met some people who, like us, had survived the flood. They told us a bus was coming to take us to the airport.

The best thing about the crowded airport was that the smell of death was finally left behind. There were people milling all around us and some strangers were there to help the refugees.

Eti talked to a group of young women, and suddenly I saw them hug my daughter and they were crying together. It was as though they knew each other.

"Oh, Mama, these people will help us get out of here. They are Christians from Jakarta who have come to help."

I was amazed. Why would people who did not know us come here to our city of death? Why were they interested in us?

We flew in an airplane to *Bulgar*. Eti's friends told us whom to ask for. When we arrived, we were taken to a large building where we could bathe and wash our clothes. There were even clothes available for those who had none. I was simply amazed by the generosity of these strangers.

"They do all this in the name of Jesus," Eti told me when I asked her why this help was given to us. "Mama, this is what is so wonderful about Christianity. Not only do we worship the Son of God, Jesus, but also His Spirit binds the believers together. I cannot imagine having gone through this without Jesus."

I knew. I saw that even though Eti had suffered like the rest of us, there was something about her that was different.

It was here that Okky found us. What a glad reunion that was! But it brought to my mind vividly that my mother was still missing. I had tried to find out something about her, but no one knew anything.

Then we went to Medan and stayed there. There, for the first time, I went with Eti and Okky to church. We all went, including

Fitri. She was really part of our family now.

I listened in amazement as the preacher talked about the tsunami. He told us that, in spite of the trouble and death and suffering it brought, God still loves us. He spoke much about Jesus, and I felt something inside of me break. I guess the terrible things we had endured made me realize how weak and frail we humans are. I agreed with the pastor that we could not do things ourselves. We needed help.

He spoke about the Christians who had died. He talked much about heaven and how wonderful it is there. He told us that only Jesus can make it possible for anyone to enter that beautiful place.

In the camp, I thought much and hard. The words I had heard in church went over and over through my head. My life felt wrecked, ruined.

I often wondered if we could ever go back to Banda Aceh. Would it ever be possible to live there again? All I could think of was the debris, the dead bodies, and the horrible stench. How could it ever be cleaned up again?

I grieved for my mother. Why had I not stayed there and helped her to safety? Would her spirit come to haunt me because of my unfaithfulness? Would the gods punish me?

The pastor told us that Jesus loves us. He is not interested in punishing people, but in saving them.

This was all so new to me. Old thoughts and old habits were still very much a part of my life. Or rather, a part of the life I used to have.

Here, there were no gods to pray to. No candles, no images of Buddha.

One day, I was sitting by myself, grieving for my mother. Eti came in to our space in the refugee camp, carrying Fifa.

"Mama, are you missing Great-grandmother?" Her voice was soft and gentle.

Tears streamed down my face. I could not speak. I was all torn up inside.

Eti sat with me, saying nothing. But I knew she was praying. I just knew it.

All that week, I felt as though my insides were crumbling. I went to church on Sunday, and during the songs, I felt as though I needed much more than I could ever get by myself. After the message, the pastor began praying and asking God to save us in the name of Jesus. He asked the Spirit to move in the hearts of those who were troubled and afraid. I knew he was praying for me. Something broke inside of me, and when people began to kneel and pray, I fell onto my knees and began crying.

"I want to change gods. I want to believe in Jesus." My thoughts were all jumbled, but I knew that Jesus truly is the Son of God.

I was so thankful for the pastor who talked with me after the service. He answered many of the questions I had.

Eti and Okky were crying too, with tears of happiness.

"I know Jesus is the real God, because I saw what He did for Eti through the tsunami," I told the pastor. "I want to have a God who is a friend. Like Eti's God."

"It is very unusual for an older woman to become a Christian," Eti told me as we talked about her mother's conversion. *"All her Buddhist friends cannot believe it and they constantly scold her for leaving her ways. Yet she remains steadfast. She tells her friends that Buddha and the household gods did nothing for her during the tsunami, and that Jesus helped her daughter."*

Today they are back in their house and the barbershop is open again for business. Eti showed me around the first floor.

"Here is where a household god was. And here. And here. When I was a child, if we so much as touched one of the gods, we had to stand in front of them, bow down, and ask the gods for forgiveness. Now they are all gone. Most of them were washed away by the flood, but those that we found under the mud were thrown away. My mother did that."

7

Hopes Drowned

"We have to go see how my sister *Mei* is doing. Her house might be completely ruined," *Ita* begged her husband. "You know their house is older than ours. They might be in trouble!"

"I tried to call them on the cell phone, but there is no answer," *Lei* said slowly. "The phone just rings."

"Come, let's go," Ita urged. "They might need help."

"We are going to check on Mei," the couple yelled across the yard to their married son. "We'll be right back."

With Ita riding on the back of the motorcycle behind her husband, they left. They headed toward the center of the city, away from the sea.

Their journey was slow. People were milling around in the street, assessing the damage the earthquake had done. A large crowd had gathered around the new supermarket that had collapsed, with only a few of the tall walls still standing among the ruins.

"Hurry!" Ita urged as Lei stopped the cycle to look at the devastation. "I am so worried."

"It will take a long time to rebuild all the houses," Lei shouted to Ita above the noise. But he gunned the cycle in response to her urgency.

With relief they entered the street where Mei lived and saw her house still standing.

"I'm okay!" Mei called out when she saw them coming. She embraced her sister when they met her on the street. "My house is still standing. Oh, what a dreadful experience that was! I thought I was going to see my house collapse right in front of me."

"Let's go back and make sure the family is all right," Ita suggested. "Our houses were damaged but nothing serious. Let's go back and check on the children."

Inwardly, Lei grinned. First they had to race over and see if Mei was all right. Now they were to race back and make sure their married son, his family, and Lei's brother and family were still fine. It would do no good to tell his wife that they were unhurt when they had left and there was no reason why that would have changed. That would not make Ita relax. It was her nature to want to stay in contact with all of their family. At least most of them lived close together, except Mei.

Obediently Lei got back on the cycle. With a wave to her sister, Ita got on the back.

When they got close to the mosque, Lei noticed something very unusual was happening. There was such a huge crowd of people rushing into the grounds that surrounded the mosque and trying to get inside that the road was completely blocked. The people were screaming and shoving.

Then he saw the wall of water rushing down the street behind the people, overtaking them and tumbling them over.

Hardly thinking, Lei made a U-turn and gunned his cycle, roaring back the way they had come. Other cycles raced along beside him, heading for higher ground.

"Oh, what is it? What is happening?" Ita was yelling in Lei's ears.

"I don't know. There must be a flood!" Lei tried to think.

"What? Oh, this is terrible!" Her grip tightened around Lei's waist. "Where do you think our family is?"

With a shake of his head, Lei did not answer. He too was worried. What could have happened? Did the city water mains break? No. There was no way that could have flooded the streets as they had seen around the mosque.

The earth continued to shake. They could see the palm trees sway back and forth, and the roofs of the two-story houses swayed back and forth as well. But none of the quakes were as severe as the one they had experienced that morning.

Coming to the edge of the city at the foothills, Lei stopped his cycle and they dismounted beside the road. Other people stood there too, looking over their city.

"A wall of water is destroying the city," a young man said loudly. "I was leaving my house on my cycle when I saw this huge wall of water rushing toward me, washing away cars and people and houses, and tumbling them into a huge mass of junk!"

"Where?" Ita asked breathlessly. "What street were you on?"

The speaker did not pause. "I saw people being thrown into the air and smashed against the walls. Babies were flying out of their mothers' arms, and I turned and raced away as fast as I could."

Ita covered her face and began to weep. "Oh, how terrible! Our family! Whatever happened to them?"

Lei tried to think. He listened to the others talking.

"We must go back!" Ita wailed. "We have to go back!"

"You can't go back," a woman told her. "The city is under water."

A sudden jolt underfoot caused panic among the small group gathered beside the road.

"Will the water come up here? Is it a tsunami?" Questions were tossed out among the anxious group. Questions, but no answers.

"There is no phone service. The towers must have been knocked over." People tried to think how they could get in contact with someone to find out what was happening in the city.

Overhead, the sun was shining brightly and some white, fluffy clouds drifted along. It was as though all the world was peaceful except for the earth beneath them. Lei marveled how the sun could continue shining when there was so much devastation all around them.

More and more people were coming out of the city. Stories of flooding and destruction came with the refugees. Lei and Ita felt their hopes sinking. Children wandered around, desolate and in shock.

Hours later, the report swept through the crowd. "The water is going down. It's going back out to the ocean."

This time, Ita did not need to urge her husband to go back and check on their family. He was on the cycle, ready to head back into the city. She climbed on behind him.

They made their way the short distance to Mei's house. The water had not touched her house.

"You can't go back!" Mei told them. "The water has taken out all the houses along the coast and the rest were flooded. Even the first floor of the mosque was flooded."

"You stay here," Lei decided, talking to Ita. "I will see how close I can get."

"Go!" Ita urged, her eyes filling with tears. "Our houses were much closer to the sea than the mosque. Oh, Lei, go quickly!"

It did not look good. Before Lei could even get close to their house, he was already driving through standing water. Everything had been covered with a thick, gooey mud. The water ran up the wheels of the cycle and drenched his clothes, yet he kept on going.

Finally the motor died. Lei got off and waded through the water, pushing his cycle. Abandoning the drowned cycle, he waded on through the knee-deep water, trying to hurry.

His progress was slow. Mud-covered debris was piled up against the stores and houses. Cars were overturned and small boats lay scattered among the wreckage.

But it was the corpses lying about that wrenched at Lei's heart—men, women, young people, and children. Crumpled up, some with missing limbs, the bodies lay sprawled among the wreckage.

One gruesome scene etched itself into Lei's mind. As he turned a corner, he saw a stack of dead bodies piled up against the side of a building, lying in an orderly fashion. The flood had caught the market-going people and piled them up like fish in a market stall. Lei turned his head and quickly walked on.

By the time he finally reached his street, his heart was beating fast and his breath was coming in short gasps, not only because walking was difficult, but also because of the terrible warlike zone he was walking through. When he finally reached his house and saw his son's house on one side and his older brother's house on the other side, all three still standing, he tried to hang on to hope.

"*Xie!*" He tried to call out loudly for his son, but only a strangled cry came out of his throat. "Xie!" he called out again, his voice stronger now.

There was no answer, just the silence of the devastation before him. There were no voices, no sounds of traffic, no children crying. Only a dead silence filled the street and swept over the weeping old man.

"Xie!" Lei's voice broke and he began to wail loudly. He began yelling the names of his brother's family, then tried his son again. He called for his daughter-in-law and he called for his grandchildren, but his echoing cry came back empty.

There was a movement on the top of a roof. Lei looked up eagerly and saw the face of his neighbor peering down at him.

"Tell me quickly! Have you seen my son? Have you seen my family?"

"They tried to get out." The words were empty, emotionless. "I saw them trying to leave on the cycle. The water hit them," he said simply. "It hit them and it hit my family too. They are all gone."

Frantically, Lei battled his way through the trash and entered his house. The bottom floor was piled high with debris, the front wall completely gone and the rear wall pushed out. He clambered up the stairs to the second floor.

Devastation was everywhere. The water had completely flooded the rooms. The windows were all gone, leaving empty staring holes in the walls. There was no sign of anyone.

Tears streaming down his face, Lei searched his son's house and then his brother's house.

His search was fruitless. There was nobody inside.

Then he began searching among the dead. Turning the faces of the dead sideways, he looked hard and long for his family.

When the evening shadows began lengthening, Lei knew he had

to return before dark. He did not want to stay in this place of death overnight. There was no home to return to, no place to stay. No electricity, no food, no water. Nothing.

He dreaded to return with no good news about their family. How would Ita survive? How would any of them ever recover? The loss of their house was great, but much, much greater was the loss of their family.

Ita wailed and buried her face in her hands as she rocked back and forth. Mei tried to comfort her sister.

"If only we would have stayed!" Ita wailed in despair. "Why did we leave? I wish we would have died with them."

Lei had no answers. There were none. "Maybe we can look again tomorrow. Perhaps they are safe in some other part of the city." He tried to offer a thread of hope.

"They would come here," Ita wailed in answer. "I know they would have come here."

The next day they left Mei's house and went from place to place where people had taken refuge, hunting for some member of their family. They met hundreds of other people doing the same, and whenever they saw some tearful reunion, hope would spring up once more in their despairing hearts. Perhaps they would find someone.

They did. One.

"Fifa! Over here," Lei suddenly cried.

His younger brother had been working his way out of a crowded room when Lei spotted him.

They were in each other's arms. Ita was sobbing uncontrollably.

"Have you seen any of the others?" Lei asked as soon as he could speak.

Fifa shook his head. "I thought all of you were dead."

Fifa had never married and lived in the center of the city. "We went upstairs to the third floor when the flood hit," he explained. "Afterwards, I couldn't get out because the floodwaters were everywhere. I had to stay in my house until the water went down. I have been looking all day for someone in the family. I went back to your house and couldn't find anybody. I wanted to get to Mei's house, but I couldn't."

In the following days, they continued their exhausting search. They spent their nights at Mei's house, and during the day they hunted for the missing. But it was all to no avail—they never found the missing members of their family.

Lei carries the photos of his family with him in his wallet. Showing me the now wrinkled and worn photographs, Lei's eyes fill with tears as he lovingly points out each member of his family. His son, his daughter-in-law, their two children. His brother, his sister-in-law, and their son. He names them one by one.

All young, most of them smiling in the pictures. All victims of the tsunami.

8

The Man on the Pole

"May I come in?"

Jesslyn looked through the partially open door at the young girl. It was *Risma*, her neighbor who attended the university in Banda Aceh.

"Yes, come in." Jesslyn opened the door wider and stood to one side to allow the girl to pass.

With a quick backward glance, Risma stepped quickly inside and Jesslyn closed the door.

"Come to the kitchen and I will make some tea." Sensing Risma's uneasiness, Jesslyn welcomed her to their house with a smile.

Silently Risma followed her hostess to the tiny kitchen. She sat down on one of the two chairs flanking a tiny table.

"*Nurdin* went to work early today," Jesslyn chatted as she set the teakettle on the stove and measured tea leaves into the pot. "He has to leave early on some days when they have to do extra framing work."

"I guess you wonder why I have come," Risma said, slowly stirring the hot tea in her cup with a spoon. "I wonder if you can help me." She lifted her large dark brown eyes from the cup and looked at Jesslyn.

"I will try," Jesslyn said. Her mind was in a whirl. Just what had brought this young Muslim girl to her apartment this early in the day? Though they had met numerous times in the stairway and in the hall that served the apartments in their building, they had not become well acquainted.

Jesslyn and Nurdin had only recently moved into the building, and it had not taken them long to realize they were the only non-Muslims on the block. There had been no open hostility at first, but as the neighbors found out that a Christian couple had moved into their building, they began to show their animosity. Jesslyn tried to be friendly to the women, but it was Nurdin who bore the brunt of the hostility. He worked with some of the neighbor men in his construction job, and they often spoke scornfully of people who had accepted the "Western religion."

So it was with great surprise that Jesslyn heard Risma asking her for help. "How may I help you?" she asked softly.

"I had a dream," Risma began. "Actually, I had many dreams. All the dreams were the same, and at first I did not really pay much attention. But as time went on and I continued to have the same dream over and over again . . . I cannot forget."

"What did you dream?"

"I saw a man being nailed to a pole by a group of rough soldiers. This man did not fight, but allowed himself to be nailed to the wood, and then the soldiers put the pole in a hole in the ground and the man hung on the pole for everyone to see." Her brown eyes shone with intensity as she related her dream. "There was a group of people, men and women, standing not far away, all dressed in white robes. They were looking at the man on the pole."

Jesslyn listened in fascination.

"I was there too, watching what was happening. I was pretty close and as I looked at the man and wondered why he was being killed, he looked directly at me. His eyes were shining and he was smiling at me! That smile amazed me. I could tell he was not angry, but somehow filled with love. I did not know it was possible for someone to be filled with love when such a dreadful thing was happening to him. Then I woke up." Risma put both hands on the table, gripping the edge, and leaned forward.

"The next night, I dreamed the same dream. I saw the man on the pole, looking at me, and again he smiled at me with love. I have never experienced something like this."

Jesslyn's heart was full. Great joy surged through her.

"Can you help me?" Risma put one hand on the front of her blouse. "Something tells me there is a meaning to these dreams. I feel as though God is talking to me about something."

"Why do you come to me?" Jesslyn asked kindly. "We hardly know each other. I mean, I am glad you came, but I am also curious why you have chosen to ask me."

"I debated a long time," Risma said, looking around the tiny kitchen. "I have heard my relatives speak against you and your husband because you are Christians, but there is something about you that I don't see in our women. I have felt drawn to you since I began having these dreams, as though maybe you were one of those people in that group dressed in white."

Jesslyn felt the prickle of tears in her eyes. She leaned toward her visitor and said, "You have met the God of the Christians. That man on the pole is Jesus Christ!"

There was silence in the room. Through the open window, the noise of cars and cycles continued to fill the street with sound, but all was still in the apartment.

"Jesus? The Western God?" There was a note of dismay in the young girl's voice.

"No," Jesslyn corrected her gently, "The Son of God. Jesus is not a Western God. He is the God of all true Christians."

"I have heard so many terrible things about this man, Jesus," Risma said hollowly. "How can He be the man in my dreams?"

"Yes, I am sure you have heard many terrible things," Jesslyn said kindly. "Not everyone who is not a Muslim or a Buddhist is a Christian, contrary to what many of you Muslims believe. Often when you hear of "Christians" who do terrible things, you immediately class everyone together. But the people who truly believe in Jesus Christ want to do the things He did when He was on earth. They believe in Him in their hearts. There is a difference."

Taking a quick look at her watch, Risma stood up. "I must go. My first class today was canceled and that is why I had time to come see you."

Jesslyn stood up too. "I am so glad you did. I will tell you how you can learn more about the man in your dreams. Would you like to know?"

Risma hesitated only for a moment. "Yes, I would."

"On Sunday, come with Nurdin and me to our meeting. You will hear the speaker talk about Jesus and you can hear much more about Him." Jesslyn held her breath.

"What time?" Risma asked. "I will come. I have to know more! Tell me where you meet."

The next Sunday, Risma did indeed come. Jesslyn had wondered all week if the young girl would keep her courage. She and Nurdin prayed daily for their neighbor.

Jesslyn rose and slipped from her seat as she saw Risma enter the room where they had gathered. She sat down beside the young girl and smiled at her.

Risma returned her smile shyly.

The next Sunday, Risma was there again. And the next. And the next.

"I understand that Jesus truly was a remarkable man," Risma told Jesslyn one Sunday after services were over. "A great prophet. The Koran teaches us that."

"Did you ever wonder if he was more than a prophet?" Jesslyn asked seriously. "Now that you have heard the real story of Christ, do you understand that He is indeed a prophet, but much, much more? He is the Son of God!"

With a sigh, Risma replied, "It is all rather confusing. I am trying to balance what I hear in the meeting with what I have been taught. I have to put away so many thoughts that I used to have about Jesus. But I really want to know the truth. I tell God that I must know. I cannot rest until I know the truth!"

Risma did not attend their meetings for several Sundays. "I'm going to other churches," she told Jesslyn. "I hear more about Jesus and I also hear other things. Sometimes I get so confused."

Jesslyn bowed her head. "I am sorry," she said softly. "There are a lot of people who go to church and there are many different ideas about how to follow Jesus. All I can say to you is that you must seek to know Him personally. He has to come into your heart and make you a new person."

Risma listened intently. "I just wish I knew," she said hopelessly. "There are so many questions running through my mind."

"Jesslyn! I—I want to talk to you."

Turning from inspecting the vegetables at the open market, Jesslyn looked toward the speaker.

It was Risma on her cycle.

"I was on my way home and saw you here," Risma told her, balancing her cycle with one foot on the ground. "Are you in a hurry?"

"No," Jesslyn replied. "I am almost finished shopping."

"Meet me at the bridge," Risma told her and, starting her cycle, she drove on down the crowded street.

"We can sit down here by the river," Risma told her when Jesslyn arrived at the bridge. "No one will see me here."

Jesslyn agreed. There were too many people who would question why a young Muslim girl was talking with her.

"I asked the priest at the church to baptize me," Risma plunged right in. "I have decided that I really do want to be a Christian."

"I am glad," Jesslyn said simply. She waited for Risma to continue.

"At first he did not know what to say. You see, when I told him my full name, he immediately knew what family line I belong to. My father is a very important political figure and I think it scared the priest. 'It may be better for you to go to the evangelicals to get baptized,' he told me.

"I was hurt. I thought he would be glad to have me convert to Christianity, but instead he told me to go somewhere else to be baptized.

111

"Well, anyway, I went to where he suggested, and that pastor told me I should go to Medan to be baptized. Medan? I don't know any Christians in Medan. So then I realized he, too, was afraid to baptize me because of who my father is. Even though my family lives thirty miles from here, he was too scared.

"I told him that I would be very careful and not let anyone know I have converted to Christianity. I would continue to dress like the Muslim women, and even when I come to church on the cycle, I would make sure no one knew where I was going. None of my friends know I am a Christian."

Jesslyn felt a sinking sensation in her heart. She looked at Risma. With sincerity she asked, "Risma, are you truly a Christian? Do you have the life of Jesus in your heart, or are you a Christian only in your head? There is a difference."

Risma met her gaze. "I want to believe in my heart," she said softly.

"I know you have visited different churches and I think you are confused. I have a suggestion. Why don't you go and visit with our pastor, *Josua*? I think he could help you with your questions, and if you really are sincere, I am sure he will baptize you. He will not turn you away."

"I will come," Risma said with conviction. "I do want to know the truth." The hot August sun shone down on them warmly, but the two women hardly felt the heat. Their hearts were burning with something far more important.

Jesslyn and Nurdin hurried into the hospital corridor, asking for directions. As they entered the women's dormitory, they saw two girls sitting beside a bed.

"She is very sick," one of them said as the couple came closer.

Jesslyn felt her eyes fill with tears as she looked at the figure lying still on the cot. Tubes ran into her arms and dark circles made half-moons under the closed eyelids. Risma really was very sick.

"We brought her in yesterday," one of Risma's classmates said. "The last several days she complained of having headaches and we kept telling her to go see a doctor. She said she didn't want to because she did not know why she was sick."

Someone else came up to the little group beside the sick girl's bed. It was Josua.

"Should we let her family know?" the taller of the two girls asked.

"We will help her," Josua said. "We will pay for the expenses. Why not wait for several days and see how she is."

The two girls shrugged their shoulders and soon left.

"She has been under terrific pressure for the last two weeks," Josua told the couple after the girls were gone. "Every night she has been coming and asking questions. My wife and I have tried to explain what being a true Christian is and I know she wants to believe. I think she does believe, yet there seems to be something keeping her back."

Bowing his head, he began praying silently. The comatose girl on the bed did not move.

Raising his head, Josua said with tears. "I may be to blame too. I had a real struggle when I heard who her family is. For days, I was afraid of what her father would do to our church if I baptize her. I hope Risma did not sense my struggle."

Jesslyn heard the anguish in the pastor's heart. She knew his fears were real, for if it would be public knowledge that a Muslim, especially from a prominent family, had converted to Christianity, there could be major repercussions. The Muslim government would look the other way as the Christians were persecuted.

"How are you feeling?" a nurse asked several days later. She smiled as she felt for Risma's pulse.

"A little better," Risma replied.

"Mmm, those flowers smell good," the nurse commented graciously as she bent over the bouquet Jesslyn had brought on one of her daily visits.

Just then a commotion at the entrance to the dormitory caused the nurse to turn her head quickly toward the disturbance.

"Risma!" A man and a woman, followed by two girls, came swiftly toward the bed.

"Father, Mother!" Risma smiled weakly. "The girls came too." Her eyes went from her parents' faces to the faces of her older sisters.

"Yes, we came," her mother said quickly. "We need to know what is going on here."

"I am sick," Risma answered *Meisy*. "They do not know what is wrong with me."

"Sick! You are sick because you allowed Christians to influence you. You ungrateful daughter." Risma could see her mom was extremely upset.

"Is it true?" Risma's sister *Henna* asked, looking at her quizzically.

"I . . . yes. Some of my Christian friends have been here. They . . . they have been good to me." Risma's eyes darted from face to face.

"Ahh!" Meisy wailed. Turning to her husband, she cried, *"Embong*, we have been betrayed. By our own daughter."

Turning back to the sick girl, she said in a hard voice, "When your school friends called and told us you were in the hospital, we asked them some questions. They gave us some unusual answers."

Risma's father cleared his throat. "Risma, surely you have not been deceived by accepting the Western god." His voice was low and tender, yet grave.

Slowly Risma closed her eyes. Her lips moved slightly. Then she looked at her family again. "In my heart, I know I must speak the truth. I believe in Jesus Christ, the Messiah for all people."

Both her sisters inhaled sharply. But Meisy sprang into action.

"You are insane," she hissed, her face contorting in anger. "We will see about that. You are coming home with us."

With a few swift movements, she undid the adhesive tape that held the IV needle in place and yanked out the needle. Signaling to Henna, she grabbed her youngest daughter and pulled her into an upright position.

Risma tried to call for help, but she felt powerless under the swift, decisive actions of her mother.

"Wait!" her father called to his wife as she and Henna half

dragged, half pulled Risma out the door. He trailed along behind, looking about for any staff.

Halfway down the stairs, Risma fainted.

"Grab her," Meisy commanded her husband, and Embong lifted his daughter in his arms.

"Into the car," Meisy ordered, and bustled them into their waiting vehicle.

" . . . she is an infidel. An unbeliever!" Risma came up out of a swirling fog to hear her grandfather speaking in shocked tones.

She opened her eyes. Taking a quick glance at her surroundings, she realized she was at home. Home, encircled by her family and relatives.

"Maybe she will recant," Embong said in a low voice. "I cannot accept that my daughter should be one of those—those despised Christians."

Risma flinched. His tone when he said "Christian" was so filled with scorn and derision that it was evident how reprehensible it was to him that one of his family should even be associated with such people. To him, Christians were dogs and outcasts.

"She is awake!" exclaimed *Yessy*, her middle sister. "I saw her move."

"Risma, tell me it is not true," Grandfather pleaded, his wrinkled face quite close to hers. "Tell me you are not a—a Christian."

Fastening her eyes on her grandfather's face, Risma replied, "Grandfather, please listen. It is not as you think. Jesus is not a Western god. He is the Son of God!"

"Blasphemy! Oi, oi, oi!" Meisy's voice broke into a loud lament. Henna and Yessy joined their mother in wailing.

"She is now a Gentile. Such a person will keep faithful Muslims from entering heaven. It is written, 'Cursed be the family of the Gentile.'" Grandfather's tones came loud and clear into the clamor.

The voices of aunts and uncles and cousins all babbled excitedly. Never had such a thing happened before. Oh, the shame and horror of the crime this young daughter had committed by consorting with the despised Christians.

"It would be better for such a one to be killed," one of the uncles broke in through the cries of the family group. "Then the way to heaven will be opened for us again."

Risma felt a strange strength go through her. She sat up in bed. The room became silent.

"I am willing to die," she said in a low, distinct voice. "I have found a faith not only worth living for, but also worth dying for. I believe that Jesus Christ is the Son of God." All eyes were fastened on Risma as she sank back onto the bed again, weak with illness.

A chorus of wails and imprecations met her declaration. "Away with her. She must be killed. Heretic! We are all doomed!" The voices clamored and filled the room.

Embong looked at his daughter and pleaded with her. "Please," he whispered. "Give up your heresy. At least until the pressure is off. You can later go back to what you believe. They will kill you!"

Once more Risma said clearly, "I believe in Jesus Christ. I am willing to die for my faith."

"She is possessed," Embong decided. "Call for *Kamto*."

Someone left the room and the rest waited.

Minutes later, a short, heavyset man entered the sickroom. Dressed in black from his turbaned head to his shoes, the man breathed heavily.

When he saw Risma, he broke into a loud chant and waved his arms over her body. Then his voice lowered and he murmured softly and slowly, weaving his hands over and under each other.

A few moments later, a priest from the mosque entered. With hard eyes, he watched Kamto at work over Risma.

"She must be bathed in water from the holy well," Kamto decided. "There are evil spirits living in her body that control the mind, and they must be washed away." He looked at Embong and raised his eyebrows.

Embong nodded. Putting his hand into his pocket, he drew out money and handed it to Kamto.

Grateful and somehow refreshed, Risma lay back down on the bed after her bath. Her mother and her sisters had chased everyone out of the room and sponged her body with water from the holy well.

Then the group reassembled. Kamto once again began his incantations, waving his hands around her and chanting in a singsong voice.

"Three spirits," he kept whispering. "There are three spirits in her. They will not let me come in."

"Bind the Holy Word onto her feet," the priest instructed. "She will be tied to the Koran."

All night long, Risma lay in bed, her feet covered with bands of fabric that tied sheets of verses from the Koran securely to the soles of her feet. She slept quite well and felt strangely rested the next morning.

When she decided she was well enough to get up, Risma discovered that not only were her feet bound by the Koran verses, she was also tied to her bed. She plucked at the fabric that bound her to the bed, but was too weak to untie the hard knots.

"Henna, come help!" Risma called.

It was not Henna who came, but her mother.

"I need to use the bathroom," Risma explained. "I am tied up."

Meisy untied the fabric strips with difficulty and, without speaking a word, helped Risma to the bathroom. Afterward, she waited until Risma was once more on the bed, then firmly tied the fabric back to the bed.

Risma did not dare ask any questions. Her mother's face was frightening.

When Yessy brought her a bowl of soup, she too remained silent. Risma could hear a commotion downstairs and the murmur of voices rose up to her bedroom.

For a week, her family left Risma in silence. After the first three days, she was no longer tied, but though Risma felt relieved at this relative freedom, she still knew she was a prisoner.

On the fourth day, her father came softly into her room in the afternoon and asked quietly, "Risma, do you still refuse to give up your faith in the Western god?"

Risma knew it was difficult for her father to even say the name of Jesus.

Her answer was clear, "I know that Jesus Christ is the Son of God. I believe in Him in my heart."

Embong did not stay long. Quietly he left the room.

"Risma!" Jesslyn drew the girl in and closed the door to their apartment. "Oh, praise God! We have been constantly in prayer for you."

"How did this happen? Come, sit down." Jesslyn led her friend to a cot in the living room. "You still don't look well," she said, looking closely at her young friend.

"I escaped," Risma said cryptically. "One day when I noticed nobody was guarding me, I got away."

"There, there," Jesslyn comforted her as Risma began to weep silently. "I will make some tea for you."

"Jesslyn, I want to be baptized. I want to seal my faith in Jesus Christ by water baptism and show first of all to God that I am a Christian and also to others that I believe in Jesus." Risma looked at Jesslyn, her eyes determined and her voice steady. "Can you call Josua for me?" she asked.

"Risma, do you believe that Jesus Christ is the Son of God?" Josua asked the young Muslim girl.

Standing waist-deep in the river beside the pastor, Risma said clearly and distinctly, "I know that Jesus Christ is God's Son."

Josua cleared his throat, and his voice was husky. "Are you willing to deny your former religion, the world, and Satan, and declare yourself a child of Jesus Christ?"

The small group of Christians on the bank of the river listened carefully. All attention was focused on the white-robed figures in the water.

"Yes, I am willing to leave my beliefs behind. I want to believe in Jesus Christ only." Her voice, still steady, carried clearly above the murmur of the river.

"Then, on the testimony of your faith in Jesus Christ, I baptize you in the name of Jesus Christ, the Son of the living God." Gently Josua lowered Risma into the water.

Someone began singing a song, and when Risma reached the shore, Jesslyn was there to welcome her. Extending her arms, she embraced the girl who had become so dear to her. Others crowded around, welcoming Risma to their fellowship.

During the day, Risma moved about from place to place. Late in the evenings, she came to Jesslyn and Nurdin's apartment and spent the nights with them.

Risma's family began a campaign to try to find their daughter and take her home with them. They harassed Jesslyn and Nurdin to the point where the couple moved into another apartment in a distant part of the city, where they remained hidden.

"We will see how long you last without money," her mother told Risma one day on the phone. "You are now on your own. You are no longer a daughter of mine!"

All financial support was withdrawn, and the young girl became dependent on her friends for her needs.

A few weeks later, she found out that her family had held a "funeral" for her. They symbolically cut her out of their lives. Taking a banana plant, they had dressed it up in Risma's clothes and buried the effigy. They told their friends that Risma had died, and they buried the banana plant and erected a tombstone with Risma's name on it.

Then, in late December, the tsunami hit.

It was evident that Risma's family still had feelings for her, especially her father, for he traveled to Banda Aceh to see if his daughter had survived.

Risma had traveled to Medan with Jesslyn and Nurdin, but she was able to speak to her father on the telephone.

"I cannot come and see you," he told her. "Your mother insists that we cut off all ties with you. If you come back into our lives, it will damn us unless you return to our faith."

Once more Risma lovingly told her father that she could not recant. She chose her faith in Jesus over her earthly family.

"Risma has a big work to do," Josua told me as he related her story. "She is from an influential Muslim family, and this may be a

way for God to use her to spread the Gospel to the Muslim community."

But Risma also knows the danger she is in. Her very life is in danger, and for now, she is keeping her whereabouts a secret.

"The tsunami has changed the minds of many people here in Banda Aceh," the pastor continued. "The Muslims have seen how many foreign missions have come into our city to help us. They are amazed that people from other countries are willing to help rebuild our city when they do not know us or share the beliefs of the Muslims.

"I pray that God can use the tsunami to further soften the hearts of these people. Risma may have a big part in this work."

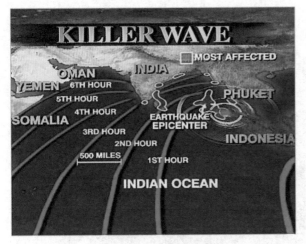

December 26, 2004:
A mighty earthquake
deep under the Indian
Ocean created a
huge tsunami wave
that traveled outward
from the epicenter,
all the way to the
African continent,
devastating 12
countries surrounding
the Indian Ocean.

This building stood three stories high before the quake.

The earthquake collapsed many buildings, trapping and crushing people inside, but the destruction wrought by the huge tsunami waves that followed was much worse.

Many houses stood no chance as the force of rushing water swept them off their foundations.

Survivors searched for bodies or something of value among the mounds of rubble.

Fishing boats washed ashore and settled on the piles of debris.

Tanker trucks tumbled in the rushing water, and many people drowned in their vehicles, unable to escape.

People say water was within 10 feet of the top of this 90 foot tower.

Some boats found strange moorings.

This huge four story high electric generating barge floated three miles inland. Because it can not be returned to the ocean, it will become a tsunami memorial.

The height and force of the wave capsized this ship.

This boat came to rest on top of a house. Fifty people found refuge in it, escaping the raging water.

This boat also was carried three miles inland into the city and came to rest in front of a large hotel.

Massive erosion affected the coastline as the water slammed against the mountainsides.

Miles of coastline were flooded and stripped.

Before and after satellite photos. Built on a peninsula, the city of Meulaboh was the second most populated area of destruction in Indonesia. After, almost everything gone; completely wiped off the land.

Photos courtesy of DigitalGlobe

A residential section of Meulaboh, before and after. Total devastation; no sign of houses or life.

Bodies and debris jammed at the bridge above. From this spot alone, 800 bodies were recovered.

Missing person posters were displayed on windows at the Banda Aceh airport.

In Banda Aceh, a city of 425,000 people, 80,000 died. This area was closest to the center of the earthquake.

Bodies were put into body bags, loaded onto trucks, hauled to mass burial sites, dumped into trenches, and buried. At the time of CAM's visit, the count at this site was 30,000.

Today that same site has become a memorial of the tsunami victims. According to government report, 50,000 bodies are buried here.

At another site, 3,200 people were buried in front of what was Meuraxa Hospital. The hospital grounds will also be developed into a tsunami memorial.

In March, two months after the tsunami, survivors started moving back onto their land, using whatever they could find among the rubble to fashion the crudest of shelters. They gathered wood scattered in the debris and built temporary houses to live in.

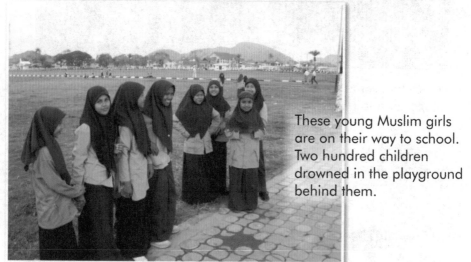

These young Muslim girls are on their way to school. Two hundred children drowned in the playground behind them.

This youngster is from the village of Deah Baro. He survived the tsunami by hanging on to a tree branch as he was caught up in the current that carried him two miles inland. God has spared his life for a purpose, from an area where almost no children survived. His family all perished. He now has been "adopted" by the village people.

CAM rebuilds in Indonesia

Temporary housing of survivors

To show the love of Christ in this Muslim area, CAM is rebuilding houses in Banda Aceh. Indonesian nationals put in the foundations, with volunteer crews from North America doing the framing, roofing, and siding.

As of September 2006, 194 houses have been built.

In addition to rebuilding houses, CAM is building an interest in the good news of the Gospel through *25 Favorite Stories of the Bible* in Indonesian. Notice their expressions as they study the picture of the crucifixion.

Volunteer workers show God's love in action

setting trusses

chow time

roofing & siding

finishing touches

9

Mercy

The earthquake, *Nasrul* knew, had unnerved them all. When he told his wife that he wanted to go see if the church building had been damaged, *Shinta* had at first begged him to not leave her and their daughter, *Herlina*. "What if another earthquake comes? Can you not wait until we see if this is over?"

"I will wait another ten minutes, then I will go," Nasrul told her. More tremors had kept him at home and had kept them from going inside to assess the damage to their modest home.

So by the time he had walked the short distance to the church house, really only two houses down, more than twenty-five minutes had gone by. He was eager to see how the sturdy church had withstood the quakes that had shaken them early that Sunday morning. Never in his life had he experienced such a quake, and he really was amazed that not more damage had been done to their city.

He was barely down the street before he knew the church house was still standing. The two-story building rose tall and secure above the smaller houses around it.

Before he got to the churchyard, Nasrul stopped with a puzzled frown wrinkling his forehead. He heard the sound of people yelling, and another, even stranger, noise. Water! Nasrul was puzzled, yet he knew the sound of water when he heard it. Like a gigantic waterfall.

He heard someone shouting, "The sea is rising!" Nasrul looked down the street and saw a group of people running toward him. Behind them was a gigantic mass of something black, a moving wall behind the people.

Nasrul dashed up the steps of the church to see better. The noise was getting louder, and even as he strained to see over the ten-foot-high wall of the church, he saw the wall fall inward right in front of his eyes.

As though pushed by a gigantic bulldozer, a pile of debris washed through the break, lumber and junk coming through with a crash.

With a cry of alarm, Nasrul dashed around the side of the church into a narrow alley. He sprinted toward the edge of the church, only to see water come spraying through a bank of debris pushed up against the alley. Hardly knowing what he was doing, he turned and splashed through ankle-deep black water toward the front of the church.

As he rounded the corner, he saw the wave of debris had washed up against the side of the church and the entire yard was filling up with water. He scrambled up the junk that already blocked the front door and felt the rubbish move under his feet. More and more debris was pushed through the opening in the churchyard wall.

Scrambling and slipping, Nasrul clambered up the pile of junk. Higher and higher the debris piled up against the side of the church. Now Nasrul was higher than the second floor windows, and still the pile beneath him kept growing. Up and up he clambered, slipping and falling more than once into the roiling water. Gasping and straining, he tried to keep his balance as his footing shifted and churned beneath him.

A green sofa came surging toward him as another wave of water pushed more debris his way. With a lunge, he grabbed hold of the upholstered arms and struggled to stay on top. As the water level continued to rise, he stood on top of the back of the sofa, grabbed the edge of the tile roof, and pulled himself up.

At first, he just lay on the sloping roof, out of breath. Then he became aware of the other people on the roof. He scanned their faces to see if he recognized anyone.

They were all strangers. Instantly his thoughts went to his family. What had happened to Shinta and Herlina? He sat up, and immediately saw a ship come sailing down what had been the street. He was bewildered. What was the ocean doing so far inland? How was it possible for this huge amount of water to be flooding the city?

Then it dawned on him. This was a tsunami, caused by the severe earthquake they had felt only thirty minutes earlier! The ocean had come and covered the shore for miles. He suddenly realized that not only their city of Banda Aceh was being flooded, but the entire coastline of Indonesia must be suffering from this calamity. Thousands of people would be affected.

"Help! Oh, help!" The cry was faint, but close by. Nasrul turned his head. A woman, moaning and clinging to wreckage, was feebly struggling to keep her head above water. Nasrul watched numbly as she was swept away, out of his reach.

It was a motley crew of refugees that had either washed up on the church house roof or somehow managed to get to relative safety. A man and what looked like his teenaged son sat on the ridge, staring dumbly into the watery graveyard around them. A bedraggled chicken, a few white feathers showing beneath the oily black scum, squatted forlornly at the edge of the roof, and a small snake coiled only a few feet from the chicken. A movement at the edge of the roof caught Nasrul's eyes, and he watched as a green frog leaped from the edge of the roof onto some debris below.

Then the shaking began again. The building beneath them rumbled and shook, and Nasrul began to pray. The only words he could think of were, "Lord Jesus, save us! Be with my wife and my daughter, wherever they are. Lord, what is to become of us? What is happening to the world?"

He tried to keep his sanity by repeating the twenty-third Psalm. "Though I walk through the valley of the shadow of death, I will fear no evil. Thy rod and thy staff, they comfort me!" Over and over, he repeated the same phrases. The promises brought a certain peace to his heart.

The roof was becoming tremendously hot in the burning sun. Nasrul tried to stay in one place rather than moving about, as the tile beneath him stayed cooler than where the sun shone full on the roof. The chicken opened its mouth and the snake lay coiled in a small circle.

"Nasrul!" He heard someone call his name. It sounded like—it *was* Shinta! Where was she?

"Nasrul, over here!" He looked toward the sound of her voice.

"Praise God!" Nasrul stood up and called to her. "Where is Herlina?"

"Right here." Shinta motioned and Herlina scrambled over the ridge top of the house roof.

"Stay there. Let me come over." Nasrul went to the edge of the roof and looked to see if there was any way across to the next house roof that was between them. Rubbish was piled high between his roof and the next.

Was the water going down? Yes! He could see a distinct line where the oily water had left its mark on the house next to the church.

"Oh, Nasrul, do be careful!" Shinta called to him. "Is it safe?" She held her hand to her mouth. Her voice sounded weak. And scared.

Nasrul walked along the edge. Rubbish was piled high against the side of the building, and he did not know how stable the piles were. Would he be able to make it to the next roof? Once on that roof, he could jump across to where his wife and daughter were.

"Oh, Jesus, save us!" Shinta began to pray. Her voice carried across the space to Nasrul and he heard her desperation.

Carefully Nasrul lay on his stomach and squirmed backward over the edge of the roof. Slowly he lowered himself toward a palm tree lodged against the side of the building. As soon as his shoe hit the trunk, he tested it by pushing against it. It felt firm, so he lowered himself onto the tree trunk, holding onto the roof with his hands.

Then the perilous journey began. Gingerly he inched his way

down the sloping trunk and across a space onto a chunk of roof that had jammed against the rubbish pile. Everything was covered with black mud and very slippery. Nasrul was getting covered with mud. He held onto anything he could to keep his balance.

A low moan from beneath a pile of rubbish startled him. He looked underneath an upturned car and saw a man, eyes wide open in his mud-covered face, staring up at him. "Help!" he wheezed.

For a moment, Nasrul paused. A shudder went through his entire body. The man was beyond help. Both of his legs had been torn off and his life was ebbing away. Nasrul felt tears sting his eyelids, and for a moment he could not continue his arduous journey. But he knew even if he should reach the man, there was no way he could help him.

Slipping and sliding, he made his way toward the neighboring house. He refused to look directly at all the corpses among the debris.

With great relief, he reached the roof and climbed up onto it. Then, jumping across the gap, he was at his wife's side.

"Are you all right? Is anyone hurt?" he asked anxiously. With relief, he saw that both his wife and teenaged daughter were not seriously hurt.

In thankfulness, all three bowed their heads in prayer. The women wept and Nasrul felt tears in his own eyes. The long hours on the rooftop by himself, expecting to find his family dead, had taken a toll on his nerves. It was almost unbelievable that they were together.

"We heard people yelling, 'Water! Water!' " Shinta told her husband. "I couldn't believe it at first, and then Herlina went up the street to see."

" 'Mama, we will drown!' I heard the panic in her voice and we raced upstairs. The water came roaring up, and when it broke the upstairs windows and poured in we ran up to the attic. From there we climbed out on the lean-to roof and then went on top of the house."

Her eyes wide in remembrance, Shinta buried her head against her husband's shoulder. "I was sure you had drowned. There were so many dead bodies floating all around. Oh, it was terrible!"

"I wanted to grab the cell phone, but I had no time," Herlina said. "I thought I could use it to call for help." She looked around the devastated cityscape. "I don't think there is anyone to call for help," she said, a sob breaking her voice.

"We are indeed among the few blessed ones," Nasrul said. "The loss of lives must surely be in the hundreds."

"What will we do?" Herlina asked nervously. She looked at the receding water, exposing more rubble than any of them would have considered imaginable before the flood. "Where will we go?"

"I want to see if we can get our papers," Nasrul said, thinking of their passports, birth certificates, and the deed to their property. "Then we will see."

It was after four o'clock before they decided to leave the rooftop. By that time the water had receded, leaving behind pools everywhere. They went back to the second floor of their house, and, to Nasrul's relief, he found the metal box with their documents safely inside.

"There is not much left to save," Shinta said, looking around the ruined living quarters. "I am sure the stove and the refrigerator do not work anymore after being in water that long."

Herlina looked disconsolately at the soggy, mud-covered furniture. "I want to get out of here," she said softly.

The stairway was completely blocked by debris. Nasrul pushed in vain against the jammed junk.

"We have to go out one of the windows," he said. "I will go first and then help you down."

He dropped down on a pile of junk, about five feet below the second story window. Then, with Herlina steadying her mother from above and Nasrul taking her feet, Shinta lowered herself out the window. Herlina's slight form was not difficult for Nasrul to guide down beside them on the rubble.

"Watch out for broken glass," Nasrul warned them. "It would be terrible to get cut by this dirty debris." His mind flashed back to the man who had lost his legs.

When he saw Shinta look toward the front of their house, he said,

"Don't even think of trying to save anything. We must leave this place and head for the mountains. All the dead bodies will bring disease." He knew it would take a long time for anyone to collect all the bodies. The task was monumental.

Working their way through the piles of rubble, they joined other survivors of the flood trying to get away from the drowned part of town. It was after six o'clock before they reached a place where many had taken refuge. The people were shaken, and compassion bound them together. Nasrul was able to get instant noodles for his family, and they ate gratefully.

At seven thirty, another shout came streaming through the crowds, "More water coming! Water!"

With cries of alarm, the crowd panicked, and many darted toward any three-story building they could see. They pushed their way inside and raced for the upper stories. People were pushed and shoved and screams of horror rose in a wave of noise.

"No!" Nasrul tried to comfort his wife and daughter. "We have not had a severe earthquake since this morning. It takes a severe earthquake to form an enormous wave."

Shinta turned tearful eyes to her husband. "I can't stand it. I am so afraid! We must get out of here."

"Let's go to the mountains," Herlina begged. "We can get to higher ground there."

Nasrul looked at the distraught women. He saw their anguish.

"Please!" Shinta begged. Her entire body was shaking in terror.

"You take Herlina and go," Nasrul decided. "I will stay, and tomorrow I will try to go back and see if our house is all right. I want to see how the people from our church fared. There is much to do. I must stay here."

Nasrul stayed in the city, and when he went back the next day to their house, he was amazed that he and his family had escaped. With greater clarity, he saw the destruction the tsunami had wreaked on the city. There was nothing salvageable in his house, and he joined the people from his church in hunting for the missing. They found thirteen bodies that were recognizable and held a quick mass burial for them.

Everything they tried to do was greatly complicated by the chaotic conditions. People began to loot and pillage what little the earthquake and tsunami had left intact. Corpses were robbed of jewelry, stores were broken into, and anything of value was carted off. These indignities were carried out in broad daylight, and lawlessness and banditry were rampant. The police were either too busy with their own catastrophes or not equipped to deal with such a calamity.

The next several days were chaotic beyond belief. Corpses were rotting in the streets and it was becoming extremely dangerous to even be in the city. The airport was mobbed with people trying to evacuate. It was there that Nasrul met the first of the aid workers.

A trickle of supplies, food, and medicine began to flow into the devastated area to help the survivors, but it was difficult for any organization to be effective as long as the piles of debris and dead bodies were rotting and spreading diseases. The air was putrid and aid workers who came to clean up became nauseated from the horrible sights and smells.

Today, a year later, Nasrul and his family are back in their repaired house. He is busy helping the people in his area get back on their feet and has a consulting business for those trying to find work or begin new businesses.

"'Though you walk through the fire, you shall not be burned.' This verse was true for my family, but there are many who cannot say that. I do not know why God has shown us mercy and spared us, but I want to show my gratefulness by being occupied in the work of the Lord," Nasrul said.

10

Story With No End

I know I am only one of many who lost their families in the tsunami. There are many orphans who now live with relatives, extended families, or in orphanages like I do. I am fifteen, on the threshold of manhood, and I have been forced to grow up and accept a changed life.

I am—or was—the oldest of three children. The only boy. I know my father expected me to take his place someday in our family. Maybe he still expects it. I don't know, for he is dead. I feel confused many days because I don't know what is expected of me anymore.

I had been up early on December 26, for I always get up early. Or I used to get up early. Now, we are not allowed to get up too early for no one is in charge then and the director says we might get in trouble if we get up before we can be supervised. Anyway, that morning, I was up and in the house with my father. We were just finishing our morning coffee and I was telling him about a dream I had.

In this dream, I had seen the ground rise way up into the air. We all were on the ground, and our houses, our street, everything, had been lifted up. It had been a strange dream. I had been on the ground, but I could see how our city of Banda Aceh was lifted up into the air. I told my father that I had been the only one to survive. I had been very, very scared.

My father had not said much about my dream, only that I must have dreamed about an earthquake and that, although we have earthquakes, we have never had such a massive quake in his memory.

It was right then that we felt the ground beneath us begin to shake. I looked at him in horror. "Just like in my dream!" I cried out.

Then the shaking got worse. "Run!" my father said, and he went into the back room to get my mother and little sister. My other sister had left the house with my aunt earlier.

We all ran outside to the road. I watched in horror as I saw our one-story, two-room house begin to crumble as it was shaken like a rat in a dog's mouth. The roof collapsed, and my mother held onto my father so he wouldn't try to run inside to grab stuff.

It was too unreal for me to understand. It was really like in my dream. The ground rose up beneath us, and as we were lifted up, the tremors sent us flying to the ground. Houses all around us were collapsing and everyone was screaming and crying. I did not know I was crying until I felt tears drip onto my bare arms folded tightly across my chest.

My mother sat on the street, rocking my baby sister and wailing and sobbing. My father stared at our house, not saying anything. On and on the ground rocked. I could see that my aunt's house right next to ours was still standing, and I began to wonder if we could move in with her once the earthquake was over. But I was not sure it would ever be over. There would be a few seconds when the ground would hold still, then the deep rumbles would begin again, and the earth would start shaking again. I noticed the palm trees were swaying and shaking. Several old trees had fallen over, the tops of the trees spread out on top of house roofs.

I really do not know what all went through my mind while we sat there. I do know I had never been so scared in my life. I was terrified, and when I heard my mother begging Allah to save us, I knew the grownups had never been this scared either.

Even now, I do not like to think about it. Those terrible memories want to come and make a big black hole in my brain. I feel all tight inside, not only because of what happened right then, but also because of what happened about thirty minutes later.

After the earth stopped shaking so much, I still had my father and my mother. Even though we didn't know what we were going to do next, I was still with my family. That meant a lot to me. I remember looking up at my father's face and thinking, "I bet my father will find a way to rebuild our house. He has always taken good care of his family." I remember how his dark brown eyes looked—sad, yet not without hope. There was a firmness about his mouth that made me respect him.

My aunt's house was still standing. "I hope they are all right," my mother said anxiously, holding my little sister to her breast tightly. I knew she was thinking of my middle sister and my aunt, Mom's sister.

The street was filled with people crying out and trying to find their relatives. I don't remember all I did. I mainly just wandered around, staring at the damage the earthquake had done to our house, our lives.

I remember wondering why some of the houses had collapsed and why some had not. It really did not make sense to me.

Our area close to the seashore was mainly one-story houses, yet there were occasional two-story houses and even some three-story houses. The damaged houses were surrounded by many buildings still standing.

There were still occasional rumbles and shakes beneath us. A strong quake had just sent us out onto the street when I heard people screaming. I looked down the street toward the sea, and screamed. A huge monster of a wave was coming right toward us! Like a black cobra rearing its ugly head, the wave crest was higher than any building.

Screaming with fear, we all began running as fast as we could to escape the wave of death. The street was full of people, screaming and running. There was no thought of what we should do. We just ran as fast as we could. My father had grabbed my baby sister and was running with her. My mother was running beside me, screaming.

Once, I looked back. Then I wished I hadn't. People were being caught by the wave and the crowd caught was tumbling over in a seething mass of arms, legs, and bodies. I ran as fast as I could. Fear lent strength to my legs and I caught up with my parents. I passed them and ran with all my might.

Then I was running in water, and I knew the wave had caught up with us. I screamed at the shock of the strength of the water and felt myself falling. I heard my mother's voice, a long piercing wail of utter despair. I felt people grab onto my clothes and I jerked away. There were people all around me, and suddenly I could no longer run. I fell down and was swept away.

So ends Hendra's story. Actually, it has not ended. He still lives his nightmares, one year later.

When we arrived at the orphanage, I was impressed by the long, low, white cement block building that housed the boys' sleeping quarters. The orphanage director and his family live in an older wooden house, repaired and painted.

"Talk to Hendra," the director told us. "He has quite a story." So we sat on the porch and began the interview. The interpreter skillfully relayed the above story.

When Hendra started telling us about running down the street away from the "cobra," his actual word, he stopped for a bit and tears formed in his eyes. I signaled to the interpreter to wait and Hendra sat beside me, trying to control his emotions.

I placed my hand briefly on his leg in sympathy and then, with an effort, he began talking again. But only for a moment.

He stopped talking and, putting his face in his hands, began to cry. Abruptly, he got up, stumbled off the porch, and with tears streaming down his face, walked around the back of the orphanage building, his shoulders shaking.

I did meet his sister, just younger than Hendra, who, when the water had hit her, managed to climb on top of a pile of rubble along with several other survivors. Evidently they were on higher ground, for they escaped and fled to the mountains. Later she and Hendra were reunited.

The rest of the family was lost. There were no near relatives, so these two were brought to the orphanage and are being raised there. Although there are hardly any girls in this orphanage, I wonder if they allowed several girls to be there so Hendra and his sister could be together.

The building was provided by a Muslim aid group and is funded by Muslims for displaced children. Their physical needs seem to be provided for, and yet I could not help but wonder who is providing for the emotional needs these young survivors experience.

11

Saved by a Miracle

My father cannot understand how it happened. Even now, he talks about the strange event that took place during the tsunami. He says there is no reasonable explanation for what happened. But I think I know what happened and why.

We were at home, my little sister and I, with my parents and my little niece, *Versilia*, who was only six months old. My married brother and his wife had left that morning to visit family on the outskirts of the city, toward the mountains. We were having so much fun with Versilia, who cooed and smiled so easily at us. It was a treat to have her stay with us. We had never had that privilege before, for her mother still nursed her. This time they decided that, rather than taking her by cycle on the hour-long trip, they would leave her with us and come back in the early afternoon.

The earthquake hit with terrific force. We all ran outside, my father holding Versilia and trying to protect her little body from falling debris. My sister, nine years old, huddled close to Mama. Even I, with all of my twenty-seven years, clung to my mother's side. We were all frightened.

I began to pray.

Mama and I had become Christians some years earlier, and our faith was very precious to us. We had not been raised in a Christian environment, and it had not been an easy step to believe that Jesus Christ is the Son of God. Not that our family had been religious— we really had not had a religion.

My father said he was an atheist and did not believe in any god, except maybe the god of nature. He claimed that no one could know for sure whether there was one god or many gods. He said if there were gods, they were not interested in helping people make a living or giving them happiness and peace. He claimed that if there were gods, they were only interested in helping themselves.

My mother and I knew better. We had experienced the love of Jesus when we had repented and believed in Him. Our lives began to have meaning and we very much enjoyed our worship services and the fellowship we began to have with other Christians. Our faith made a huge impact in our daily lives. We still had to work hard to make a living, and our faith did not make us rich. My father never let us forget that.

Nevertheless, we now had Someone to turn to in our troubles. We had learned that, in our most difficult trials, if we prayed to God, we no longer had to carry those problems. We could let Him take care of the things beyond our control.

That is why, when the earthquake began shaking us so violently, I immediately began to pray. I knew where to go when there was no place to go. Jesus was my refuge.

Mama began praying out loud, and I joined her. It was reassuring, with the earth rocking beneath us and the houses creaking and groaning, to know that one thing had not changed. Jesus Christ is always the same.

I could hear my father mutter beneath his breath. I felt his anger toward what was happening. I prayed harder.

"Lord, if you choose to come and take us home to heaven, let it be so. You have told us you would come for your bride, the church of Jesus Christ, and if it is now, we are ready."

The cries of the people all around us indicated that they too were praying, each according to his faith. The Muslims were crying and wailing to Allah. The Buddhists were praying to the only god they knew—the cold statue of a man who was dead and had no power to help anyone.

I think I may have been praying more for Father than anything else during that earthquake. For so long now, I had been asking God to break through the hard shell around my father's heart. For over two years, I had felt a burden for my father's salvation. I loved him very much, yet I sensed the anger and resentment that seethed in his life. He loudly complained about his lot in life and often lashed out with angry words toward his family. I knew he loved us, but he was a slave to his feelings.

More than once, when I found Father lying asleep on the cot after a hard day's work, I had softly crept over and gently placed my hands on him, praying for his repentance. I never told anyone, and he never knew what I was doing. These prayers gave action to the longing in my heart, and I felt the Spirit moved me to do this. Of course, I also prayed for him other times, yet it was during those times when I could actually pray over my father that I really felt he would someday repent.

The people at church helped my mother and me tremendously. They knew how we longed to see my father become a Christian. They often prayed with us for his salvation.

So now, when the earthquake erupted all around us, I immediately began praying for my father.

"Lord, you know how to speak to all of us. If you choose to speak to my father through this shaking of the earth's foundation, do so. Make yourself known to him."

When the ground had quieted down, my father got up and walked around, holding his little granddaughter tightly against his chest.

Versilia was the delight of her grandfather's heart. He doted on his grandchild and spent a lot of time holding her and playing with her. There was something about the little girl that brought out a very tender part of him. We used to tease him that he loved her better than he loved the rest of us. But we were all glad to see how much he adored her, and we did not mind the love and attention he lavished on her.

When the wave came sweeping into our city, everyone instinctively tried to escape. There was not a lot of time to think what would be the best way to save ourselves or help others. We just acted. We look back now and wonder why we didn't do this or that or look out for each other more. But at the time, everything happened too fast. We had been standing out on the street, and when the wave came rushing toward us, we all just ran.

Right next to our house was the Buddhist temple—a massive, solid, two-story building. Taking my little sister by the hand, I ran with my mother into the courtyard and we scurried up the steps. The water began swirling around our feet before we had quite reached the second floor.

"Where is Father? And Versilia?" Mama gasped, all out of breath. We ran to the windows to see if we could see them.

The street outside was filled with water, almost up to the second floor windows. We could see people floundering on wreckage, trying to stay afloat in the black, oily water. The screams of the injured echoed strangely through the flooded streets. A babble of voices behind us came from other people who had taken refuge in the temple.

"Mother, I think it is the end of the world!" The words just sprang from my mouth. "How will this be? We have read and talked about it so much. Now it is happening. Remember, the Bible says that before the end of the world there will be earthquakes in different places. Then destruction will come. Jesus will come back for us!" There was a strange feeling of excitement in my heart.

We knelt on the floor and all three of us began praying. Occasionally we would begin to sing. Our hearts were full, ready, and expectant. Beneath us, the temple shook as more quakes rocked the foundations.

"You have promised you will never leave nor forsake us. We claim that promise in the name of Jesus Christ, the Saviour, our King. We love you, Lord Jesus, and we commit our lives into your hands." Words of praise welled up from deep inside our hearts.

Part of me wanted to know what was happening around us, and I faintly wondered where Father and Versilia were. But at the moment, I was caught up in the Spirit and all earthly things became vague and dim. I fully expected to see Jesus coming with His angels to take us home with Him.

I know we waited several hours upstairs in the temple, praying and singing with each other. It was a precious time, and even though we felt the fear and tension from the other people there, we felt secure in our trust of the living God. We knew He was right there with us.

Then, suddenly, Father was there! Dripping wet and covered with grime, he was clutching something in his arms. Something moving.

With cries of joy, we sprang to our feet and rushed over to where he was standing. Versilia's eyes were frightened, but she was not crying. She was all right.

"I don't know how it happened. It still seems impossible!" In a daze, my father kept repeating these words over and over again.

"Use my jacket to wrap her in dry clothes," I urged, handing him my still-dry jacket. My mother took Versilia, undressed her, and wrapped her in my jacket.

"Let me hold her again," Father said, reaching for her. "I still don't know how it happened. I thought I had lost her."

The story came out as we sat on the floor of the temple. We were barely aware that the water level was receding outside as Father told us what had happened.

"When the wave came, I was right outside *Bonar's* cycle shop. I ran into the shop and headed for the stairs, along with several other people.

"Before I could get upstairs, the water hit us with a rush and knocked me off my feet. I flew against the wall, and as the water surged around me, I realized Versilia was gone!" Tears flowed down Father's cheeks as he gazed at his little granddaughter.

"I was frantic and tried to see where she had gone, but a woman blocked the way and would not let me go back down. The water was still rising and I panicked. I began calling, 'Versilia!' hoping I could see her. I even felt under the dirty water with my hands, but I only found junk. I thought for sure she had drowned."

Tenderly he laid his cheek against the chubby face of Versilia. We were all in tears as we thought of the little baby somewhere under the water.

"Where was she?" my little sister asked with wide eyes.

"I ran upstairs, almost beside myself," Father continued. "I went over to the window and looked out, crying loudly. I thought my heart was breaking. I saw bodies being washed past the window, and every time a child or baby was washed past, I looked to see if it was Versilia." Father stroked the baby's damp hair.

"Then suddenly, there she was! Floating, coming right toward the window where I was!" Father's tears flowed faster. "She was floating right on top of the water. The current sent her right toward me and I reached out and plucked her right off the top of the water. It is a miracle! It is a miracle!" He could speak no more.

Mama and I began praising God. Our thankful hearts overflowed and we prayed and prayed as we wept together. Somehow, God had seen fit to spare our dear little Versilia.

That evening, Versilia's parents found us and heard the wonderful story. They, too, were Christians, and we prayed together in joy. God had spared our entire family, even little Versilia.

By then, I realized that God had not ended life on the earth, but He had spoken in a mighty voice and made us all aware of His great power and might. For some reason, He had not come to take all His children home. He was giving sinners another opportunity to repent.

In our prayers and conversations later, Father was strangely silent. He did not scoff or rebuff us when we talked about how God had saved little Versilia with a miracle. He was deep in thought.

There was a lot of activity the next several days. We tried to salvage what we could out of our flooded first story and carry it safely to the second floor. Not that it really helped, because later, after we had been airlifted to Jakarta, thieves broke in and looted anything of value. We did not have much, but they ransacked the house.

Two days after the flood, we were in Jakarta. Our relatives there were very helpful and gave us what we needed. Although their house was crowded with seven extra people, we were happy to have a place to stay. Banda Aceh had become a polluted place of rotting corpses and decaying vegetation.

When we went to church, I invited Father to go along. At first, he did not say anything. He just looked down at his feet. "All right," he finally answered, his voice low and husky, "I'll go with you." With hearts full of joy and gratitude, we walked together down the city sidewalk toward the church.

The song service was wonderful. The church was packed, for not only did many Christian refugees come, but people from Jakarta had also experienced much loss from the earthquakes and many people were turning to the Lord. We lifted our voices in song, and as we stood and praised God together, many wept. The mighty hand of God had touched Indonesia.

God's hand also touched my father. During the song service, the Spirit touched my father's heart and I saw him begin to cry. He wept for his sins and for the wonderful love God had shown Him.

Today he is a changed man. He prays with us and goes with us to church. After we returned to Banda Aceh, he was baptized.

He still talks about the time when little Versilia came floating toward him in the flood. "It is not reasonable that anything like that should happen. There she was, just floating along, and she came straight to the window where I was. It truly is a miracle from God! I cannot understand it."

Me? I think it was the way God chose to speak to my father's heart. I think God wanted to show my father that He is in control of everything, and He really cares for people. In spite of the devastation and loss of the flood, God saw the anguish of my father's heart when he thought he had lost his little granddaughter.

My father now thanks God for allowing the tsunami to occur. In spite of our personal loss and the devastation our city endured, my father is grateful for the opportunity to have become a believer in Jesus Christ.

Glossary

Acehnese	(Ah-CHAY-nese)	**Medan**	(MAY-dahn)
Aida	(Ida)	**Mei**	(MAY)
Atika	(Ah-TIK-kah)	**Meisy**	(Macy)
Banda Aceh	(BONN-dah AH-chay)	**Nalita**	(Nah-LEE-tah)
Bonar	(BOE-nahr)	**Nasrul**	(NUSS-rule)
Bulgar	(BULL-gahr)	**Nurdin**	(NOO-er-din)
Cahya	(CHAH-yah)	**Okky**	(AWK-ee)
Chicha	(CHEE-chah)	**Paristo**	(Pa-RIS-toe)
Dani	(Donny)	**Parto**	(PAHR-toe)
Dono	(DOE-noh)	**Purnama**	(Poo-er-NAH-mah)
Edo	(Ae-doe)	**Ridha**	(RID-dah)
Embong	(M-bohng)	**Risma**	(RISS-mah)
Erman	(AIR-mahn)	**Sadei**	(Sah-DAY-ee)
Eti	(EH-tee)	**Senno**	(SENN-oh)
Fifa	(FEE-fah)	**Shinta**	(SHIN-tah)
Fitri	(FIT-ree)	**Sinar**	(See-NAR)
Ghanda	(GUN-dah)	**Sugi**	(SOO-gee)
Hendra	(HEN-drah)	**Sumiyem**	(SOO-mee-ye[r]m)
Henna	(Hannah)	**Susilo**	(Soo-SEE-loe)
Herlina	(Hair-LEE-nah)	**Sutomo**	(Soo-TOE-moe)
Ita	(EE-tah)	**Ternate**	(Tur-NAH-tay)
Jakarta	(Jah-KAHR-tah)	**Venna**	(FAN-nah)
Josua	(JOE-swah)	**Versilia**	(Fur-SEE-liyah)
Kamto	(KAHM-toe)	**Vivi**	(FEE-fee)
Lei	(LAY)	**Xie**	(SHEE-ay)
Lusi	(Lucy)	**Yessy**	(YES-ee)
Manado	(mah-NAH-doe)	**Yunita**	(Yoo-NEE-tah)
Mangasa	(Mah-NGAH-sah)		

About the Author

Harvey Yoder is the author of nine previous books, including *Not in Despair* published by Christian Light Publications in Harrisonburg, Virginia. Harvey travels all around the globe gathering information for his books. Although he encounters many interesting people, he is most inspired by the Christians he meets all over the world. In spite of all our different customs, traditions and languages, we serve the same Jesus Christ.

Harvey and his wife, Karen (Anderson), have five children and three grandchildren, and live near the Blue Ridge Parkway in the scenic mountains of western North Carolina.

Christian Aid Ministries

Christian Aid Ministries (CAM) was founded in 1981 as a nonprofit, tax-exempt, 501(c)(3) organization. Our primary purpose is to provide a trustworthy, efficient channel for Amish, Mennonite, and other conservative Anabaptist groups and individuals to minister to physical and spiritual needs around the world.

Annually, CAM distributes 15-20 million pounds of food, clothing, medicines, seeds, Bibles, *Favorite Stories from the Bible*, and other Christian literature. Most of the aid goes to needy children/orphans and Christian families. The main purposes of giving material aid are to help and encourage God's people and to bring the Gospel to a lost and dying world.

CAM's international headquarters are in Berlin, Ohio. CAM has a 55,000 sq. ft. distribution center in Ephrata, Pennsylvania, where food parcels are packed, and other relief shipments are organized. Next to the distribution center is our meat canning facility. CAM is also associated with seven clothing centers—located in Indiana, Iowa, Illinois, Maryland, Pennsylvania, West Virginia and Ontario, Canada—where clothing, footwear, comforters, and fabric is received, sorted, and prepared for shipment overseas.

CAM has staff, warehouses, and distribution networks in Romania, Moldova, Ukraine, Haiti, Nicaragua, and Liberia. Through our International-Crisis program, we also help victims of famine, war, and natural disasters throughout the world. In the USA, volunteers organized under our Disaster-Response-Services program help rebuild in lower-income communities devastated by natural disasters such as floods, tornadoes, or hurricanes. We operate an orphanage and dairy farm in Romania, medical clinics in Haiti and Nicaragua, and hold Bible-teaching seminars in Eastern Europe and Nicaragua.

CAM's ultimate goal is to glorify God and enlarge His kingdom. ". . . whatsoever ye do, do all to the glory of God" (1 Corinthians 10:31).

CAM is controlled by a 12-member Board of Directors and operated by a 3-member Executive Committee. The organizational structure includes an Audit Review Committee, Executive Council, Ministerial Committee, several Support Committees, and department managers.

Aside from management personnel and secretarial staff, volunteers do most of the work at CAM's warehouses. Each year, volunteers at our warehouses and on Disaster-Response-Services projects donate approximately 100,000 hours.

CAM issues an annual, audited financial statement to its entire mailing list (statements are also available upon request). Fund-raising and non-aid administrative expenses are kept as low as possible. Usually these expenses are about one percent of income, which includes cash and donated items in kind.

For more information or to sign up for CAM's monthly newsletter, please write or call:

Christian Aid Ministries
P.O. Box 360
Berlin, OH 44610
Phone: 330-893-2428
Fax: 330-893-2305

Additional books
from Christian Aid Ministries

God Knows My Size!
by Harvey Yoder

Raised in communist Romania, Silvia Tarniceriu struggled to believe in God. But His direct answer to her earnest prayer convinced Silvia that God is real, and that He knows all about her. This book is excellent for family reading time.

251 pages $10.99

They Would Not Be Silent
by Harvey Yoder

In this book, each of the stories about Christians under communism are unique, yet one mutual thread runs throughout—They Would Not Be Silent concerning their devotion to the Lord Jesus.

231 pages $10.99

They Would Not Be Moved
by Harvey Yoder

A sequel to They Would Not Be Silent, this book contains more true stories about Christians who did not lose courage under the cruel hand of communism. It is our prayer that the moving stories will encourage you, help you to be a little stronger in your faith in the Lord Jesus Christ, and more thankful for the freedoms we enjoy in our country.

208 pages $10.99

Elena—Strengthened Through Trials
by Harvey Yoder

Born into a poor Christian family in communist Romania, harsh treatment at a state boarding school, and harassment from authorities for helping in secret Bible distribution . . . Elena finally decides to flee her home country. Will she make it? A true story.

240 pages $10.99

Where Little Ones Cry

by Harvey Yoder

This is a story about war in Liberia. In the midst of the terror that war brings are the little children. Their stories, a few of which are captured in this book, are not of typical, carefree children. Some of these true accounts have happy endings, but sad trails lead them there. The purpose of this book is not to entertain, but to help you appreciate our blessed country more and create awareness of the pain and spiritual darkness that abound in much of Africa.

168 pages plus 16-page color picture section $10.99

Wang Ping's Sacrifice

by Harvey Yoder

The true stories in this book vividly portray the house church in China and the individuals at its heart. Read how the church—strong, flourishing, and faithful in spite of persecution—is made up of real people with real battles. Witness their heartaches and triumphs, and find your own faith strengthened and refreshed.

191 pages $10.99

A Small Price to Pay

by Harvey Yoder

Living in the Soviet Union under cruel, atheistic communism and growing up during World War II, young Mikhail Khorev saw much suffering and death. Often homeless and near starvation, he struggled to believe in God's love. This inspiring story of how Mikhail grew to be a man of God, willing to suffer prison for the God who loved him, will move you to tears and strengthen your faith. You, too, will come to realize that everything we can give to the Christ who saves us is still . . . A Small Price to Pay.

247 pages $11.99

Tears of the Rain

by Ruth Ann Stelfox

The moving story of a missionary family struggling to help some of the poorest people in the world—the men, women, and children of war-torn Liberia. Vividly descriptive and poignantly honest, this story will have you laughing on one page and crying on the next.

479 pages $13.99

QTY.	ITEM		TOTAL
	Tsunami!	Reg. *$11.99*	
	Tears of the Rain	Reg. *$13.99*	
	A Small Price to Pay	Reg. *$11.99*	
	Wang Ping's Sacrifice	Reg. *$10.99*	
	Where Little Ones Cry	Reg. *$10.99*	
	Elena	Reg. *$10.99*	
	They Would Not Be Moved	Reg. *$10.99*	
	They Would Not Be Silent	Reg. *$10.99*	
	God Knows My Size!	Reg. *$10.99*	

Book total	
*Shipping & Handling	
Subtotal	
OH Residents Add 6.5% Sales Tax, PA Residents Add 6% Sales Tax to subtotal	
Grand Total	

* Shipping & Handling - USA

$0 to $10. . . . . $3.00	$10.01 to $25.00. . . . . . . $4.00
$25.01 to $55.00. . . . . $6.00	$55.01 and up. . . . . 10% of total

All foreign orders, including Canada please write or call for your postage costs.

Method of Payment:

❑ Check (please make check payable to TGS International)

❑ Visa/Master Card

Name on Card_____

Card #_____ Exp Date___/___

Signature_____

Billing Address:

Name_____

Address_____

City_____ State_____ Zip_____

Phone (_____)_____

Shipping Address (if different from billing address):

Name_____

Address_____

City_____ State_____ Zip_____

TGS International
P.O. Box 355 Berlin, Ohio 44610
*Bookstores and Dealers, please
call for quantity discounts.*

To place an order or if you
have any questions, call
Phone: (330) 893-2428
Fax: (330) 893-2305